WELLNESS
YOUR INVITATION TO FULL LIFE

by John J. Pilch, Ph. D.

WINSTON PRESS

To my dad,
my late mother,
and Jean, my wife

Library of Congress Catalog Card Number: 80-53558
ISBN: 0-86683-758-2 (previously ISBN: 0-03-059062-0)

Printed in the United States of America
5 4 3 2

Winston Press, Inc., 430 Oak Grove, Minneapolis, MN 55403

CONTENTS

68529

PREFACE

This book is about wellness and spiritual values.

There are five key elements in my concept of wellness:

- knowing the purpose and meaning of life;
- identifying life's authentic, satisfying, fulfilling human joys and pleasures;
- accepting responsibility for freedom of self-determination in life;
- finding an appropriate source of motivation (for me personally and in this book, spiritual values and/or religious beliefs);
- accepting the need for change in life, the need for ongoing "conversion."

Thus, wellness is a way of living, a life-style that consciously and reflexively centers around these five elements.

You could be terminally ill, mentally retarded, permanently disabled (perhaps even a "nerd") and still have a high level of wellness. Or, conversely, you could be a glowing picture of physical and mental health but not have the foggiest notion of a direction in life, and therefore have a very low level or no level of wellness.

To cast it into a formal definition, wellness is an ever-expanding experience of pleasurable and purposeful living which you and I, especially as motivated by spiritual values and religious beliefs, create and direct for ourselves in any way we choose.

This book's chapters refine the concept of wellness, distinguish it from health, and argue for a legitimate role for spiritual values and religious beliefs in the pursuit of wellness. Near the end of the book I present two sets of reflection questions which I use in wellness retreats to help participants understand the notion of wellness, determine the level of wellness possessed or desired, and develop a personal program for a wellness life-style. There is, finally, a list of readings and resources.

This is only the beginning; the rest is up to you.

INTRODUCTION

> We have two or three great moving experiences in
> our lives—experiences so great and moving that it
> doesn't seem at the time that anyone else has been
> so caught up and pounded and dazzled and
> astonished and beaten and broken and rescued and
> illuminated and rewarded and humbled in just that
> way ever before. Then we learn our trade, well or
> less well, and we tell our two or three stories—each
> time in a disguise—maybe ten times, maybe a
> hundred, as long as people will listen.
>
> —F. Scott Fitzgerald[1]

In November, 1975, when I was singing with the
Milwaukee Florentine Opera Company Chorus in final
staging rehearsals for *The Flying Dutchman*, I came down
with a very bad cold. Over-the-counter remedies had
lost effectiveness, and my nasal passages became
completely congested. So I took the problem to my
physician, who said she would have no trouble helping
clear the passages and conquering the cold. In the
process, a routine check of my blood pressure produced
rather high readings, possibly explained by the cold.

Consequently, after the successful production of the
opera, I returned for another blood-pressure check and
additional tests, only to discover that I had a case of
mild essential hypertension, or a tendency to high blood
pressure. Like most hypertensives I was skeptical since I

felt basically fine, but I followed her medical advice and began to read about hypertension.

The medical diagnosis "essential" hypertension means that my high blood pressure has no medically discernible cause. "Mild" means that my readings are not as high as those of others. The physician's medical treatments were minimal; she prudently prescribed the lowest effective amount of medication.

But I began to search for possible non-physical causes or explanations for my bouts of high blood pressure. The search did not have to go far afield. It became immediately apparent that many factors in day-to-day living cause my blood pressure to rise: frustrating traffic jams on the express(?)way, unfulfilling work experiences, atrocious homilies at liturgies. The conclusion was obvious: While my physician could treat my symptom (high blood pressure), only I could treat the real problems.

Singing with the opera company was a more relaxing and rejuvenating part of my day, but it was not a major portion of my life. On another occasion when the company was preparing a production of *Lucia di Lammermoor* with Beverly Sills as guest artist, I thought to myself as I stood with fifty-nine other choristers around her on stage: "How enviable! We in the chorus sing for enjoyment and insist on squeezing in this pleasure for two or three hours an evening at the end of a ho-hum or even exasperating day. But Sills does this for a living; she gets paid for what she enjoys doing. Why can't we all have this privilege?"

Then I realized that we could: Each of us can do what we want in life. We can take responsibility for our lives. It may not be easy. It may require sacrifices. But it can be done, and it will bring real happiness.

The options open to me were clear. First, I would have to accept the fact that there is no escaping stress in human life. Whoever thinks there is no stress in life has died but doesn't know it. The challenge is to identify and distinguish "good" stress (*eu*stress) from "bad" stress (*dis*tress).[2] For me, singing in the opera is eustress, a good stressful situation. A moving, convincing stage production flows from the stress of the performers; for most performers this stress begins just before the curtain rises and slowly subsides after the final curtain has fallen and the performer has gone on to the cast party.

But distressful situations (or perhaps more accurately, a bad response to a stressful situation) is one that lies in the pit of your stomach, tightening and churning, as you drive to your hated eight-to-five bureaucratic paper-shuffling mindless job; it remains with you after work through "attitude-adjustment hour," supper, and prime-time TV; it stays with you through a restless night, and has turned to burning acid in your stomach as you sit down to Maalox and breakfast. For me, the well-paying, fringe-benefit-laden, daily job that put bread on the table was also providing acid stomach, high blood pressure, and—I now discovered—an enlarged heart.

That's when the second option became clear to me. There are two possible and commendable reactions to stress: fight (euphemistically known as "coping") or flight (pejoratively described as "copping out"). I could try to learn how to cope with these stresses without getting *dis*tressed about them. Or I could admit frankly that "coping" wasn't working and turn elsewhere to look for or create *eu*stressful (i.e., healthily stressful) situations—fulfilling and satisfying living conditions for myself. I selected this latter option, even while realizing that I needed to maintain basic coping skills for life-situations that required coping because they could not be changed.

Medical treatment reduced the size of my enlarged heart. I also made significant changes in my personal life—changes which, in general, meant taking more control of responsibility for my own life and activities. At the same time, I continued to read and explore traditional and non-traditional literature on high blood pressure. This literature took me through self-help, self-care, holistic health, and finally into wellness.

It was all interesting and quite new to me, but as yet unfocused. My hypertension was not due to lack of exercise, to being overweight, to eating junk food; yet much of the literature dwelt on these topics. My hypertension was my symptom, not my problem, but the literature assumed it was the problem. Then one day I began reading John W. Travis's *Wellness Workbook*[3] and worked my way slowly through his logical, orderly, and quite different approach to wellness. As I turned one of the pages my eyes met the bold print title: "Purpose in Life Test."[4] I was puzzled. Who would seek purpose-in-life answers from medicine? As I read the questions on this test, an insight suddenly occurred. "Why, the Hebrew sage Qoheleth did something like this nearly 2000 years ago!" And I felt just like St. Francis when he turned up the gospel passages on following Jesus as he looked in the Bible for a direction for his life: "Why, this is what I've been looking for! This is what I want with all my heart!"

This insight was "one of those great moving experiences" that Fitzgerald described above. In a flash my life experiences, my quest, my unintegrated collection of information and data came together into a meaningful though as yet unarticulated or developed understanding. Travis's definition of wellness as "an ever-expanding experience of purposeful, enjoyable living—an experience which you create and direct through [a list of thirteen suggested attitudes and actions]"[5] served as a good working definition for me. His acceptance of the spiritual dimension as part of the whole person pleased me too. (But see chapter 2, near the beginning, for an unfavorable comment of his—and a reply.)

Yet something was missing. None of the wellness writers and promoters familiar to me really paid serious attention to the spiritual aspect of human beings. Most often they used the word *spiritual* as a synonym for *psychological*. As a trained biblical scholar, I intuited a clear and authentic relationship between wellness concepts and concepts in the Jewish and Christian traditions. But I couldn't find this in any wellness literature.

At the same time, as a health planner and faculty member in a medical school, I continued to discover that agnostic and even atheistic scientists in this generally secular environment in which I circulated also cherished human, spiritual values that related quite well to the wellness message I was beginning to articulate.

And so I decided to modify Travis's definition by attending to my discoveries and reformulating my definition of wellness as "an ever-expanding experience of pleasurable and purposeful living which you and I, especially as motivated by spiritual values and religious beliefs, create and direct for ourselves in any way we choose." I use the word *spiritual* in a deliberately ambivalent way in this book. For agnostics, I use the word in a humanistic sense. For those who profess a definite set of religious beliefs, I use the word in a religious sense. In this book, too, when I speak of religious beliefs I focus on the Jewish and Christian religious traditions only because I know them best. Wellness developed under another religious inspiration will have a different shape, to be sure. That is the beauty of wellness: It is eminently personal, and thereby uniquely distinctive.

This book represents the "first telling" of my story of wellness, or to follow Fitzgerald more closely, the first guise in which I've "disguised" my story.[6] The purpose of this "first telling" is to show that spiritual values (religious or humanistic) and religious beliefs (for instance, Judaism and Christianity) can (and for my life really do) serve as a basis for wellness. In the first two chapters I present my understanding of the relationship of wellness to health, religion, and spirituality. In the next two chapters I focus upon two key elements in my concept of wellness: life's purpose, and life's pleasures. The concluding chapter sketches the opportunities for wellness that fill every phase of human life. Then I present two "reflection guides"—two sets of questions intended to stimulate the reader's further development of a uniquely personal wellness concept and life-style. These reflection guides have proved popular in wellness retreats with a wide variety of groups.

I am indebted, as I have mentioned, to John W. Travis, M.D., M.P.H., whose writings on wellness provided the occasion for my great moving experience. But I am perhaps even more indebted to all my teachers, friends, and relatives who long ago made wellness impressions on me so strong that they could be revived at this stage of my life. Deserving special mention are my father and late mother and my wife Jean, who at different points in life affirmed and asserted what I believe to be a singularly effective approach to a wellness life-style: spiritual values and religious beliefs.

NOTES

1. F. Scott Fitzgerald, "One Hundred False Starts," in *Afternoon of an Author*, ed. A. Mizener (New York: Charles Scribner's Sons, 1957), pp. 131-36.

2. Hans Selye, in *Stress Without Distress* (Philadelphia: J. B. Lippincott Co., 1974), both coined and popularized this distinction.

3. John W. Travis, M.D., M.P.H., *Wellness Workbook* (Wellness Resource Center, 42 Miller Avenue, Mill Valley, CA 94941, 1977). Travis's work is in constant evolution; he may no longer hold all the ideas that have influenced me at the time of writing this book. I report him as I read and understood him in 1978.

4. *Purpose in Life Test*, James C. Crumbaugh, Ph. D., and Leonard T. Maholick, M.D. Available from Psychometric Affiliates, P.O. Box 3167, Munster, IN 46321, 1977.

5. Travis, p. 2.

6. Since writing this story of wellness, I have applied it to ministry in *Ministry and Wellness: A Holistic Approach*, NCR Cassettes, P.O. Box 281, Kansas City, MO. 64141; to spirituality in "Developing an Holistic Spirituality," a module in *Religious Enrichment by Extension*, available from the University of the South, Sewanee, TN 37375; and to other areas of life such as family, the workplace, and children.

CHAPTER ONE

RELIGION, HEALTH, AND WELLNESS

In the beginning was Religion,
and one of the purposes of Religion was to heal.
Through the course of centuries it came to pass
that healing by the priests of Religion was given
over to healing by the physicians of Medicine.
Thus did a new Religion arise: the Medical Religion.
Some of its practitioners specialized in the body
and its organs;
Others specialized in the mind and its proper
working.
As for the priests of the old Religion, their ministry of
healing was replaced by a ministry of consolation
in sickness and preparation for death.
In these latter days, voices have been heard
in the land crying:
"Cannot Religion go beyond consolation?
Is there not more than that for Religion to do in
health care?"

2 WELLNESS

This chapter will briefly sketch the relationship between religion, health, and wellness as I understand that relationship on the basis of my education (formal and informal), training, and experience in those three areas.[1] The chapter should also clarify why and how I believe that religious values can play an important role in wellness. At the same time, it should become clear why I believe that humanistic values similar to those drawn from religion can also play a significant role in wellness.

IN THE BEGINNING . . . .

Ever since humanity began, it has been concerned about health and well-being. It was believed that health was in the hands of the gods, and this belief often determined humankind's behavior toward the gods. In Greece, for instance, there is the myth of Asclepius. (The following sketch of Asclepius's life combines elements found in the three principal versions of his myth: Hesiod's, Pindar's, and Apollodorus's.[2]) Born of the god Apollo and the human virgin Arsinoe (or Coronis), Asclepius lived on earth as a god-man. In his youth he learned about medicine and cures from Chiron. Healing became his chief occupation in life.

So proficient did he become at healing that he began to raise people from the dead. (One version of his myth claims that he accepted money for raising a dead person). In any case, Zeus became angry and slew him. The disconsolate Apollo besought Zeus to take pity on his grief, and so Zeus resurrected Asclepius and declared him patron god of healing.

The followers of Asclepius continued a ministry of healing in conjunction with their venerated Master. Healing was a highly regarded aspect of popular Greek religion. The sick person came to a temple (always built near running waters) dedicated to Asclepius and followed the instructions of the priests of Asclepius.

After a ritual bath of purification, the sick petitioner went to sleep in hopes that during a dream in the night Asclepius would appear, diagnose the ill, and prescribe a remedy that would work a cure. The expectations of many were fulfilled.

In time, the priests began to assume a greater role, particularly in interpreting more complex dreams. Healings continued to occur. Crutches, canes, and other paraphernalia no longer needed by petitioners were left behind in testimony to the cures. The movement remained vigorous and flourished in the Middle East from about the fifth century before the birth of Christ to the second century of the Common Era.

Two characteristics of this form of religious healing should be noted: (1) It was not necessary to believe in Asclepius to be healed (plaques testify to the cure of cynical, skeptical, and even unbelieving petitioners). (2) The healings were generally specifistic; i.e., specific organs or parts of the body were involved. Indeed, some of the plaques recording a cure were shaped like the affected and healed organ.

Jesus the Healer
Readers of the gospels know that Jesus is presented as a teacher and healer (see Luke's famous phrase in Acts 1:1—"all that Jesus did and taught"—to describe the contents of his gospel). Many contemporary biblical scholars have demonstrated that the healing miracle stories about Jesus recorded in the four gospels appear to have been intentionally modeled upon the stories about Asclepius and other healers popular in the ancient world.[3] This does not mean that the stories about Jesus were fabricated but that the healing activity of Jesus which resembled the activity of Asclepius was narrated in the same story format. Even the origins of Jesus as recounted in the Infancy narratives of Matthew and Luke bear some similarities to the origins of Asclepius.

Without doubt, then, an important part of the life of
Jesus was his ministry of healing.

The followers of Jesus also shared in his healing
abilities (Matthew 10:1) and continued his ministry of
healing after his death and resurrection (Acts 3:1-10).
Indeed, healing has remained throughout the centuries
an integral part of Christian belief. For instance, the rite
for the sacrament known in the Catholic church as
Anointing of the Sick prays for the restoration of
health, as do many blessings in the book of rituals.
Consider also the long-standing popular belief in such
healing shrines as Lourdes.

Nevertheless, two characteristics distinguish Jesus
from Asclepius.

(1) Faith in Jesus was at least sometimes a requisite
for healing. "Rabboni," the blind man said, "I want to
see." Jesus said in reply, "Be on your way! Your faith
has healed you" (Mark 10:46-52; compare Matthew 8:13,
and contrast Mark 6:5-6 and Luke 4:14-30).

(2) Jesus appeared to heal the whole person, not just
one organ or a specific malady. This is suggested by his
frequent declaration of forgiveness of sins in conjunction
with a healing. Considering this contrast with Asclepius,
it is no wonder that the early writers of the Christian
Church viewed the cult of Asclepius as a major threat
to faith in Jesus. While a comparison of Asclepius and
Jesus made Jesus credible to the gentile reader and could
serve as a starting point for discussing the special
significance of Jesus, the same comparison involved some
risks. If one could be healed by Asclepius without
believing in him, why bother to turn to Jesus, who
sometimes seemed to require faith?

Rabbi Ḥanina ben Dosa

The Jewish tradition, too, has a long history of
experiencing healings, but obviously the Jews could not
believe in the healer as a god-man. In Exodus 15:26

they read: "I, the LORD, am your healer [literally: your physician]." This caused a certain ambiguous feeling toward human healers (see Sirach—Ecclesiasticus—38), but there were a number of holy men in Judaism known as healers.

Rabbi Ḥanina ben Dosa is one of the most famous healers in the Jewish tradition. He lived at approximately the same time as Jesus of Nazareth (from 20 to 70 of the Common Era), and many stories about his deeds are recorded in the Talmud. Here is a story from the tractate Berakot (34b) of the Babylonian Talmud:

> Our rabbis say, once upon a time Rabban Gamliel's son got sick. He sent two men of learning to R. Ḥanina ben Dosa to beg mercy from God concerning the son. Ḥanina saw them coming and went to a room upstairs, and asked mercy from God concerning the boy. When he came back down he said to them, "Go; the fever has left him." They said to him, "What, are you a prophet?" He replied: "I am not a prophet nor am I the son of a prophet. But this I have received from tradition: If my prayer of intercession flows unhesitatingly from my mouth, I know it will be answered; and if not, I know it will be rejected." They sat down and wrote the exact moment he said this, and when they returned to Rabban Gamliel he said to them: "By the Temple service, you are neither too early nor too late, for this is what happened: in that very moment, the fever left him and he asked for water!"

The story is quite similar to one told about Jesus (the centurion's servant: Matthew 8:5-13; Luke 7:1-10). But there are two significant items to note about Ḥanina in this as well as in the stories of other healings. (1) The healings are brought about by the power of intercessory prayer offered by a holy person. (2) The healing appears to be holistic. In this story, Ḥanina prayed for mercy for the boy; at his prayer the fever left him. The whole person was restored to health.

The purpose of the comparison of Asclepius, Jesus, and Ḥanina is simply to illustrate the common origins of healing in religion. No matter what your religious beliefs, it is very likely that healing has a place in their history. The comparison also prompts another consideration. You might want to pursue additional details to search out not only further commonalities but also the singular distinctiveness of great religious healers from the past. My comments do not intend to deny any uniqueness, but they do suggest that the uniqueness may not be as simple or obvious as many believers have thought. But that is the result of what happened in history.

AND IT CAME TO PASS . . . .

Through the centuries, religions continued to play a major role in health concerns and healings, while the "rational" modes of dealing with these same problems remained ever in the background. In the seventeenth and eighteenth centuries, however, new understandings of pain emerged which gave religions and medicine new and distinct roles.[4] Prior to that time, the opinions of Aristotle and Galen had prevailed. Pain, these men taught (and the majority of people believed), was felt by the sentient *soul* which is coextensive with the body; hence the illusion that the body feels pain. It is the soul that feels pain and recognizes it as evil, a result of the defectiveness of nature. Pain cannot be removed but serves only as an occasion for philosophizing on the meaning and value of suffering. Hence the primacy of religion and philosophy.

Descartes changed all this. By persuasively teaching

a separation between body and soul, he was able to convince many that it was not the soul but the body that felt pain. Pain is therefore good, he argued; it is nature's way of signaling problems. Leibniz went still further and said that, contrary to earlier belief, pain is actually a sign of the perfect order of nature. The subsequent physico-theological literature concluded that nature is governed by and functions according to eternal, necessary, and inviolable laws in which pain is the guardian and protector of life.

This new understanding of pain and suffering shifted the common belief systems and proved to be a mixed blessing. On the one hand, it gave rational approaches to health a legitimacy and a welcome role in human life. It also marked the establishment of the medical religion.[5] On the other hand, in the former understanding of pain and suffering, religion was able to help individuals explore the meaning of pain and suffering in life. This was no longer possible, since the common question no longer was "What does pain mean?" or "Why do I suffer?" but rather "When will medicine learn how to remove my pain?" Where pain and suffering remained, religion, which was no longer expected to heal, could only console. "Smile, God loves you!"; "Suffer for the poor souls in purgatory"; "Offer it up"; "Have a spirit of sacrifice"—these are but some of the expressions of consolation familiar today. Even folk wisdom reflected these attitudes when it suggested: "What can't be cured is best endured." And when consolation was no longer appropriate, religion was expected finally to prepare the person for death, which medicine could not postpone.

IN THE LATTER DAYS . . . .

Medicine has made exciting advances since the seventeenth and eighteenth centuries. Few health problems have been able to resist for long its ever-developing skills. In the judgment of many lay people, the successes of medical care have earned it, notably in America, the status of religion. Physicians are often popularly esteemed to be (like) God. Because of these experiences, the shortcomings and failures of medicine have been difficult to accept.

Contemporary authors such as Rick Carlson have addressed the shortcomings of medicine by pointing out that medicine has an "end," i.e., a limit, beyond which much can still be done to improve health. Considering that the top ten causes of death in the United States are for the most part attributable to health-defeating lifestyle rather than to infectious disease, Carlson's point about the limitations of medicine makes sense. It also raises the question whether religion might not be able to do more than console people in sickness and prepare them for inevitable death when medicine has reached its limits. Is it possible for religion to have a positive effect on health and well-being all throughout life? In this book I will present my affirmative answer to these questions. The accompanying chart should prove helpful in understanding the present health-care system in the United States and in offering a conceptual framework for integrating both religion and wellness into that system.

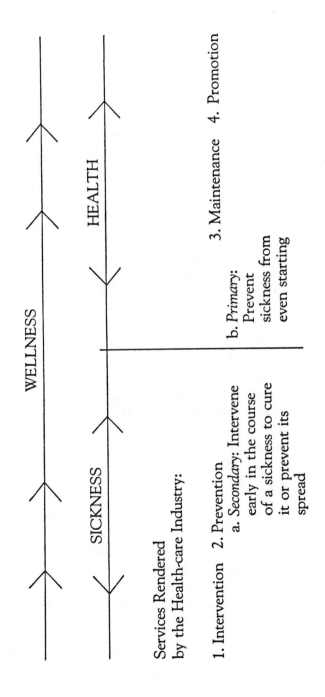

THE RELATIONSHIP OF WELLNESS
TO HEALTH AND SICKNESS

SICKNESS   WELLNESS

HEALTH

Services Rendered
by the Health-care Industry:

1. Intervention   2. Prevention   3. Maintenance   4. Promotion
                  a. *Secondary*: Intervene   b. *Primary*:
                     early in the course   Prevent
                     of a sickness to cure   sickness from
                     it or prevent its   even starting
                     spread

Jane and Joe live their lives on various points along the sickness/health spectrum. Similarly, they live their lives on various points along the wellness spectrum. The fact that I represent sickness/health and wellness by parallel lines illustrates that I, together with other wellness promoters,[6] distinguish between these realities. You can be terminally ill, mentally retarded, permanently disabled, and yet have a high level of wellness. On the other hand, you can be a glowing picture of health but have not even the foggiest notion of life's purpose or meaning, and therefore have no level of wellness. (More about this later.)

For the present, situate Jane and Joe on different parts of the sickness/health spectrum and consider what the health-care system can offer, and then what religion can offer. After we complete the lower (sickness/health) line, we will consider the upper (wellness) line.

Sickness

To begin with, notice that the lower line on the chart is divided between sickness and health. All human beings, the medical-care system, and quite definitely health-insurance companies, distinguish between sickness and health. Their criteria may differ, and the precise dividing point will be different, but in Western science, Western logic, and Western daily living nobody identifies health and sickness. You simply cannot be healthy and sick at the same time.

When Jane or Joe is sick, the medical system intervenes—sometimes when asked, sometimes (as in emergencies) when not asked. Its most familiar interventions are surgery and chemotherapy (pills, drugs, for example).

There is no question that medical care in general and American medicine in particular are a real blessing for humanity: Their approaches to sickness are quite effective and very often restore the individual to good health.

Religion, too, has a response to sickness. Since the eighteenth century its response has generally been one of consolation. And like medicine, religion has done its job well. Christian religions, for example, promote appreciation of the redemptive value of suffering, explain the relationship of sickness and suffering to participation in the paschal mystery, and when necessary prepare patients to cope with dying and death. Judaism's Book of Job offers advice on suffering. Also, today many ministers and rabbis are better prepared than formerly for their role in health care through specialized Clinical Pastoral Training programs around the country.

Yet there are two kinds of "intervention" on the sickness side of the life-spectrum in which religion might explore expanding its role: healing, and ethics.

Nearly all religions have a place for healing in their belief system. Rather than view healing as outdated or unscientific, religions might review their respective traditions in order to restore healing dimensions to prominence.[7] Catholics recently revised their sacramental rituals and even renamed the former "Extreme Unction" (directed toward preparing for death) to "Anointing of the Sick" (directed toward restoring the person to health and wholeness). This was not something new but rather a restoration of the original intent and purpose of the anointing. (See James 5:14-16.)

Judaism too has its traditions regarding communal responsibility for the sick, but it wasn't until the time of the *shtetl* (a Yiddish word deriving from the German word *Stadt*, a little town), beginning in the seventeenth century, that Jewish communities in Eastern Europe designed and maintained a remarkably comprehensive medical care program for themselves. The *shtetl* was a predominantly (and sometimes exclusively) Jewish community, usually called a "ghetto" by non-Jews.

For two hundred years this kind of care flourished.

It provided residents of the *shtetl* with spiritual, social, religious support, along with medicine and care by a physician. The services of the physician were rewarded variously in different communities. Some gave the physician a home but no salary; some gave a salary but left living arrangements to the physician. But an outstanding dimension of care in the *shtetl* was the visitation of the sick. While visiting the sick was an obligation on each individual, some *shtetlach* (plural of *shtetl*) organized societies specifically for that purpose, to be certain that the obligation would be in fact met.

Visiting the sick person involved at least three duties: cheering the patient and encouraging him or her to get better, which would also entail seeing that the physician's instructions were obeyed; cooking, cleaning and doing any other such needed tasks; and praying for the person's recovery. The warmth and comprehensiveness of this system diminished over centuries, but signs of its restoration in these days appear with increasing frequency.

Another area of intervention in sickness where religion might examine its conscience and raise a stronger voice is the area of ethics. Granted, as some physicians have noted, there may be as many "ethics" as there are "religions," but it will no longer suffice to use this fact for ignoring ethics entirely or for substituting the technological imperative ("We *can* do it, therefore we *must* do it") for ethics. If medicine has not been as sensitive to ethical questions in recent discussion as might be desired, it could be because religions have not been as vocal as they could be or have focused too narrowly on single issues to the neglect of others.[8]

There is yet one other aspect of the medical response to sickness that we must consider, because while its name may sound as if it refers to health care, it does refer to sickness as well: prevention. (See the chart.) There are at least two aspects to prevention, and one of them belongs more properly to the area of sickness.

Secondary prevention is that effort whereby the medical care system attempts to identify sickness or disease that has already begun so that steps can be taken to prevent the situation from worsening and perhaps even to restore the person to health. Examples of secondary prevention would be chest x-rays to detect cancer or other respiratory problems in an early stage, and various diagnostic tests which have the same purpose—e.g., tests for V.D. Such tests don't prevent V.D., but they can detect it early for proper treatment. Lead-poisoning screening in children is also a secondary preventive measure. Secondary prevention is a major concern in the health-care industry and one which is done quite effectively if citizens conscientiously take advantage of these opportunities. That, unfortunately, is not the case, and here religion can certainly do more to motivate people to take greater responsibility for their personal health. Religion could, for example, contribute to secondary prevention (stopping things from spreading) in the area of family or marriage problems as well as in purely physical health problems.[9]

Health
You might be surprised to see "primary prevention" on the health side of our chart. The fact is, primary prevention (preventing disease or sickness from happening, from beginning) is done to, for, and even *by* healthy persons. It is in fact an area in which medicine actually does not, and perhaps—considering the huge expense of anything medicine does—should not do very much. In primary prevention, the averge lay person is king (or queen).

The most familiar example of primary prevention in medicine is the various immunizations given to newborn babes in their first months and years of life to protect them from diseases that have proven fatal to children in the past. A recent and rare example of primary prevention among adults was the innoculation against swine flu. (Even though some elderly persons unfortunately died as a result of the innoculation that was supposed to protect them, the program nevertheless is an example of primary prevention.)

Two less recognized but very real promoters of primary prevention are the garbage men, who protect us from rats and disease by removing and destroying garbage regularly; and paint manufacturers, who have invented lead-free paints so that children won't run the risk of poisoning when they suck on toys, cribs, and other objects. Flossing your teeth is primary prevention against tooth damage and decay; getting a filling is secondary prevention; i.e., the dentist drills into a decayed tooth in time to stop the decay from spreading and requiring an extraction.

Finally, the fact that nine of the ten top causes of death in the adult population are non-infectious but rather are caused by excessive eating of proper and improper foods, by excessive smoking, excessive drinking of tea and coffee and alcohol, by lack of exercise and unmanaged stress, leads to the conclusion that primary prevention is quite clearly a personal, individual responsibility.

"Maintenance" and "promotion" of health (two terms very familiar from health-education programs) require even less medical participation and medical skill, though medical and health professionals have offered solid guidance. Both Canada (in its *New Perspective on the Health of Canadians*) and the United States (in its *Forward Plan for Health* and *Healthy People: The Surgeon General's Report on Health Promotion and Disease Prevention*) rely on medical expertise in addressing the critical role of life-style in preventing sickness, maintaining and promoting good health.

Promotion of continued good health, in fact, is quite difficult to identify in medicine and government. Physicians are frequently irritated by visits from healthy clients who mistakenly think something might be wrong. They often chide such persons for stealing precious time that could be better spent with the truly sick. Perhaps the only healthy people medicine attends to are healthy babies. Given the nature of contemporary Western medical training and practice, these attitudes and positions are understandable. Promotion of continued good health would therefore appear to be beyond the limits of medicine.[10]

Religion appears to have fared no better in this area of prevention, maintenance, and promotion. Religious bazaars and carnivals still conduct raffles for "baskets of cheer" (liquor and wines), and various congregations still sponsor "smokers" to raise funds for such praiseworthy ends as buying new equipment for the youth athletic program, or new camping equipment for the Scouts. The ironic contrast would be humorous if it were not so tragic: engaging in health-defeating practices to support health-promoting activities.[11]

Yet religion can play at least two important roles in helping prevent sickness and maintain and promote health: It can be involved in holistic approaches to health care, and it can encourage responsible political action. The W. K. Kellogg Foundation has sponsored two holistic health-care clinics in the Greater Chicago area, located in churches and staffed by multi-disciplinary teams which always include a trained clinical pastoral counselor. The underlying assumption of these centers is that many contemporary ailments can be attributed to stress and that religion can play a significant role in helping individuals cope with the stressful experiences in their lives. Wherever religion is involved in holistic approaches to health care, however, it must guard against becoming subordinated to the medical approaches (as has occurred in some instances). Such subordination sets the relationship of medicine and religion back to the seventeenth and eighteenth centuries. The holistic approach to health care requires a partnership rather than a subordination of one to the other.[12]

Subordination is difficult to avoid, however, considering the great respect paid to specialization in American society. Increasing numbers of health professionals are recognizing the holistic nature of the person: that the individual is a totality greater than the sum of all his or her parts. But the holistic approach to health care still continues to think that by representing specialists for all the parts, the whole person will be attended. Religion should work harder to emphasize that while the team approach is a good idea, each member of the team must be a "holistic" individual too. In religious settings (for example, a Methodist hospital) this would mean that each team member should have a well developed spiritual dimension, whether it is based solely on a humanistic perspective or rooted in some religious tradition.[13]

One other potential role for religion in the area of preventing sickness and maintaining and promoting health is training for political action. The praiseworthy concerns of government for improving citizen life-style and its emphasis on self-responsibility all too often become subtle ways of blaming the victims. It is difficult to believe that the government really wants citizens to reduce cigarette smoking when the same government continues to subsidize tobacco growers. Religions with prophetic traditions, such as Judaism or Christianity, should review the role and activity of prophets (such as Isaiah or Jesus) as religious critics of social situations and draw appropriate conclusions for contemporary situations in which health-conducive environments are highly desirable.

Wellness

On my chart I have represented wellness as a line (or a dimension of life) parallel to sickness and health. Wellness is not the far end of the health line; that is, it is not a superior condition of health. Nor is wellness something that necessarily leads to health. In some instances it could do so, but generally it doesn't.

Wellness is a way of living, a life-style, which centers about five key elements, as I mentioned in the Preface:

- knowing the purpose and meaning of life;
- identifying life's authentic, satisfying, fulfilling human joys and pleasures;
- accepting responsibility for freedom of self-determination in life;
- finding an appropriate source of motivation (for me and in this book, spiritual values and/or religious beliefs);
- accepting the need for change in life, the need for on-going "conversion."

I define wellness as an ever-expanding experience of pleasurable and purposeful living which you and I, especially as motivated by spiritual values and religious beliefs, create and direct for ourselves in any way we choose.

According to this understanding, you can be terminally ill, mentally retarded, permanently disabled (perhaps even "flaky") and still have a high level of wellness. Individuals in "Make Today Count" programs (groups of terminally ill individuals) can and more often than not actually do possess a very high level of wellness. Groups such as these constitute my most frequent sponsoring bodies.

On the other hand, you can be an Olympic gold-medal winner capturing every medal in your specialty but be unable to get along with any fellow Olympians. In other words, you can be the epitome of health but not have any level of wellness. You can come out of your physician's office "fit as a fiddle" or "healthy as a horse" but then go home and beat your spouse or abuse your children with all your health and strength. Healthy? Unquestionably. Well? Not at all!

Nor is wellness a synonym for mental health. True, some people who possess good mental health can also possess wellness. But it is equally true that some people who are judged (informally by a neighbor with whom they don't get along, or even scientifically) as mentally ill, mentally unhealthy, "minus habens," weird, "whacko," or flaky, could nevertheless very possibly have a high level of wellness on the basis of the five elements listed above.

Wellness is also not synonymous with positive thinking. There are times, for instance, when positive thinking won't help. Then, with Woodie Hall, we'd realize *The Power of Negative Thinking*. In fact, there is a way in which cancer specialists Dr. and Mrs. Simonton use a form of negative thinking with their patients to work toward a cure for their cancers.

Clearly, then, I distinguish wellness from health. To begin with, health is something you can do for yourself, as well as something someone else can do for you. A surgeon can return your ailing heart muscle to health by performing bypass surgery. Wellness, on the other hand, is entirely self-created and self-directed. "You alone do it, but you don't do it alone." There is no wellness practitioner but you, the individual person. Thus, well-baby clinics, as I have pointed out, are examples of primary prevention (something you can do for another) and not of wellness, since babies do not yet have freedom of self-determination.

A second characteristic of wellness is that it can coexist with chronic illness, disease, and even terminal illness, since it extends to and includes non-physical aspects of life. But health—by any definition—cannot coexist with illness or disease.

A third characteristic of wellness is that wellness is a process ("an ever-expanding experience"): It never ends. By contrast, even when health is defined as a process, it has a terminal point in the sense that there is a definite line at which one passes from health to sickness or vice versa. When that point is reached (sickness to health, for instance) the health professional has nothing more to do. "Health" insurance pays for no more benefits. When you're healthy, you've arrived. With wellness, you never arrive. You're always in process, living pleasurably and with purpose and meaning in sickness and in health.

Finally, the process of wellness is at the same time a goal. That is, we can possess wellness even while pursuing higher levels of it. Health may also be a goal, but it doesn't seem to be satisfying in itself except perhaps for a brief time after you've lost your health and regained it. A TV commercial says "When you have your health, you have everything." But more often than not, if that is all you have, you may feel you have nothing.

Health is considered more often than not as a means to a goal: e.g., keeping a job, enjoying your favorite athletic activity.[14] If you have good health but lose your job, chances are you might lose your health, too. But if you have wellness and lose your job, you will most likely not lose any wellness, for according to the definition of wellness you will respond to this challenge as an opportunity to grow in strength and maturity and to reconsider your understanding of life's purposes. You are not likely to view joblessness as an unfair and insoluble problem.

While physicians have written about wellness and have gone into wellness education, these same physicians point out that wellness is not the common

vocation of a physician and should not be expected
from the medical or health professions. It was the
discovery of a "Purpose in Life Test" in the *Wellness
Workbook* of Dr. John Travis that suggested to me that
religion could be a powerful motivating factor to
wellness, since religion (as well as philosophy and other
disciplines) surely offers insights into life's purposes and
pleasures.

Wellness education, in fact, could be a unique
contribution to contemporary society because it can not
only enhance and promote good health but can also
speak tellingly to those who do not possess good health
or have any hope of achieving it. If various religious
congregations could return to their true identity as
"caring communities"—in the spirit of the Jewish
shtetl—wellness could accomplish what health educators
and others have failed for so long to do: motivate self-
determination. I believe much the same could be
accomplished by fidelity to the humanistic philosophical
viewpoint.

Not long ago, an employer who had some workers
on his payroll who were more than 100 pounds
overweight was frustrated because they were unable to
bring themselves back to normal, healthy weight. He
then offered them $4 a pound for every pound they
would lose until they reached ideal weight. It worked!

Unfortunately, the employer was not motivated by
altruism. He worried about the impact his workers'
health problems might have on the insurance premiums
he was paying as a fringe benefit. Four dollars a pound
was a worthwhile economic gamble for him. What is
worse, the workers could be motivated by nothing other
than money. Their appearance, their health, their
stamina, the limitations of obesity—nothing convinced
them so persuasively as $4 a pound.

Yet I believe that spirituality, whether drawn from
a humanistic philosophy or a religious tradition, can do

a much better and more efficient job of motivation than money. I see this as a major contribution of spirituality to wellness. In the following chapter I explain what I mean by spirituality and suggest ways in which it can contribute to the establishment of a wellness life-style.

In subsequent chapters I show how religious beliefs and spiritual values can help you to re-examine and re-define the true purpose of your life, to find joy in life, to establish and pursue life-long wellness for yourself, and to lay its foundations for others.

NOTES

1. The content of this chapter has been amplified and developed in an audio-cassette program of mine, *Reading the New Testament Healing Texts* (Kansas City, Mo.: NCR Cassettes, 1978). Related print materials I have also authored are "Toward Understanding Miracles in the Bible," *The Bible Today* 90 (April 1977): 1207-12; and "Setting the 'Biblical Miracles' in Focus," in *PACE* 7 (Professional Approaches to Christian Education), April 1977.

2. For details see Emma J. and Ludwig Edelstein, *Asclepius: A Collection and Interpretation of the Testimonies*, 2 volumes (Baltimore: Johns Hopkins Press, 1945). The relationship of this material to Jesus is masterfully pointed out by Paul J. Achtmeier, "Miracles and the Historical Jesus: Mark 9:14-29," *Catholic Biblical Quarterly* 37 (1975): 471-91.

3. Vatican II (*Dogmatic Constitution on Divine Revelation*), especially in n. 12, summed up, approved, and encouraged the standard and common approach to scientific study of the Scripture: ". . . the interpreter of sacred Scripture, in order to clearly see what God wanted to communicate to us, should carefully investigate what meaning the sacred writers really intended, and what God wanted to manifest by means of their words." Review the article by Achtmeier cited above in note 2.

4. For this insight, see Richard Toellner, "Die Umbewertung des Schmerzes im 17. Jahrhundert in ihren Voraussetzungen und Folgen" ("The Revaluation of Pain in the Seventeenth Century: Its Presuppositions and Its Consequences") *Medizinhistorisches Journal* 6 (1971): 36-44.

5. Clifford Geertz, "Religion as a Cultural System," in *Anthropological Approaches to the Study of Religion*, Michel Banton, ed. (New York: Prayer Publishers, Inc., 1966), p. 4, defines religion as "a system of symbols which acts to establish powerful, pervasive, and long-lasting moods and motivations in men by formulating conceptions of a general order of existence and clothing these conceptions with such an aura of factuality that the moods and motivations seem uniquely realistic." In an unpublished presentation at the annual meeting of the American Academy of Religion in Chicago, October, 1975, entitled "The Health Industry

in the United States: An American Religion?" I applied Geertz's definition and delineation of elements of a religion to the health-care industry and medicine to illustrate that it does indeed constitute a "religion" in the American mind and in American daily life. For a similar conclusion by means of a different approach, see Thomas Szasz, M.D., *The Theology of Medicine* (New York: Harper & Row, 1977), pp. 146-47: "In short, medicine now functions as a state religion much as, for example, Roman Catholicism did in medieval Spain." For yet another approach, see Eliot Freidson, M.D., *Profession of Medicine* (New York: Dodd, Mead & Co., 1970).

6. See, for example, the similar parallel line schema in John W. Travis, M.D., M.P.H., *Wellness Inventory* (Wellness Resource Center, 42 Miller Avenue, Mill Valley, CA 94941).

7. The place of health concerns in Christian Science and the Seventh Day Adventist programs is quite well known. The work of Oral Roberts and his "City of Hope" project is especially challenging and worth following as it develops, because Roberts seems indeed to be pursuing the kind of role for religion in healing that I have in mind. Healing in and by religion (as in Oral Roberts' ministry) is obviously a complex and very political matter.

8. See the May 5, 1980, "Declaration on Euthanasia" by the Sacred Congregation for the Doctrine of the Faith, *Origins* 10 (1980): 154-57. This pronouncement on the use of sophisticated medical technology where there is no hope for cure, but only for prolonging life, is an example of the kind of role religion might begin to exercise with increasing frequency and vigor.

9. See ROA Filmstrips, *Christian Family* program, especially the General Introduction Guide under the heading "Rationale," for an application of this conceptual framework to marriage and family life, as suggested by the U.S. Catholic Bishops' Plan of Pastoral Action for Family Ministry.

10. Rick J. Carlson, *The End of Medicine* (New York: Wiley, 1975), has argued the case well, though in fairness to him he claims to have changed his mind about at least half of this book since its publication. He hasn't backtracked, but his developments are still in article form. Perhaps a book will be available soon.

11. Since writing this material and collecting many church

bulletins from all over the country to substantiate it, I must single out St. Roman's Parish in Milwaukee, Wisconsin, which in May of 1980 advertised a "Smokeless Smoker" entitled "No Butts About It!" St. Roman's should be granted the first "Parish Wellness" award.

12. See my suggestions in "Catholic Health Care: Roles for Laity, Religious, and Clergy," in *The Linacre Quarterly* (Summer 1980).

13. The schema presented on page 9 and this subsequent development is discussed in the audio-cassette program *Ministry and Wellness: A Holistic Approach*, chiefly on the cassette "Holistic Health Care and Preventive Medicine." The program is accompanied by pertinent bibliographies and charts. (See note 6 of the Introduction for full reference.)

14. See James Vargiu and Naomi Remen, "What Is Health For? Human Priorities in Health Care," *Western Journal of Medicine* 131 (1979): 471-72.

CHAPTER TWO

WELLNESS AND SPIRITUALITY

Spirituality is a distinctive characteristic of the human
person. Humans can relate to and respond to spiritual
realities because a person is more than a body; a human
being is a spirit, too. No matter how you choose to
specify this spirit, most people agree that it is a "higher"
element in the human person. By its nature, this spirit
possesses absolute and infinite expectancy and reaches
out to satisfy its yearnings. And it does so through the
human body, notably the senses. "Thus," observes Karl
Rahner, "the human spirit is not 'pure spirit' but
essentially a 'spiritual soul' whose ties with the
body—and therefore with space and time—make it the
specifically 'human spirit.' "[1]

    Now, when I use the word *spirituality* in this book, I
refer to that aspect of a person's relationship with
spiritual realities—or with the Holy, the Other—which
seeks to develop and perfect the human spirit together
with and *never* in neglect of or in scorn of the human

body and its senses. The task of any authentic spirituality, whether humanistic or specifically religious, is to increasingly integrate the sensuous into the whole person so that it is directed by good decisions and ordered to the Holy—to God, if you will. A spirituality that is not sensuous is not an authentic spirituality.

I firmly believe that spirituality can be a distinctive and very fulfilling element in a wellness life-style. For what could contribute more appropriately to "purposeful and enjoyable living" than a spirituality that involves the total person: body, mind, and spirit?

As a matter of fact, there are wellness programs in the U.S.A. that appear to have successfully included spiritual values and concepts in their programs. Meadowlark, for example, some one hundred miles southeast of Los Angeles, is headed by a physician of Quaker background, Dr. Evarts Loomis. His program explicitly attempts to combine religion and medicine along with other elements, and he encourages individuals to take up some form of spiritual refreshment. Clients who have visited Meadowlark view it as a way-station for spiritual journeys.[2]

In the San Francisco area, the Wholistic Health and Nutritional Institute (WHN) offers multidisciplinary therapies, including an optional and supplemental evaluation by a staff clairvoyant who is available for spiritual consultation. This staff person assists the client in reviewing the client's state of physical, emotional, and spiritual affairs from a distinctively spiritual perspective. A particularly noteworthy practice at WHN is the encouragement of guided group fasting as a practice for liberating the spirit. Christians surely recognize this as a familiar—even if underemphasized or neglected—aspect of their faith.

There are some, though, who object to a spirituality that is specifically religious in the sense that it springs from an organized religion. Some claim that religion only harms people, that it leads to poor mental health which in turn affects physical health. One such person is the psychiatrist-author Thomas Szasz. In his *Myth of Mental Illness*, Szasz asserts that Jewish and Christian religious teachings abound in rules that reward sickness, malingering, poverty and fearfulness while they penalize self-reliance, competence, effectiveness, and pride in health and well-being. He bases his claims on two points: (1) his observation of the actual behavior of persons professing to be religious (which allows him to infer the rules that govern and explain their conduct); and (2) his socio-psychological (as contrasted with literary and theological) interpretations of religious rules as he reads those rules in the Scriptures.

I believe Szasz is quite mistaken. To begin with, it is as misguided for Szasz to infer rules of conduct from the actual behaviors of *patients* as it would be for a podiatrist to generalize about the condition of the feet of all human beings on the basis of his or her private practice. In both cases, it is not the healthy that seek services, but the sick. People like Szasz may be quite accurate in their judgment about the role of religious rules in the lives of their *sick* patients, but what can they say about the role of religion in the lives of *healthy* people (who constitute about seventy percent of the U.S. population)? Whatever they say must be verifiable by the rules of the sciences for ascertaining and evaluating popular opinions.

Secondly, Szasz regularly criticizes the Scriptures, but he does not appear to quote from the Jewish Scriptures at all, while his citations from the Christian Scriptures are selective and are reported in complete disregard for literary, historical, or cultural context—a posture he would never assume in criticizing medical literature of a different time and clime. Further, not only does he arbitrarily select English biblical texts, but he also retranslates and reinterprets them in a way that does violence to the English from which he works and is not supported by the Greek and Hebrew which he ignores.[4]

Of course, Szasz anticipates criticism and rejects it beforehand by saying that since theologians are in the business of selling religion they will obviously present their case in the best possible light. On the contrary, theologians are scientists: Any theologian worthy of the name argues on the basis of objective evidence, just as physicians do in their field.

Szasz is undeniably correct in his observation that some—perhaps even all—of his patients have been harmed by religion. Who hasn't met the children of a broken family whose parents were often advised by a pastoral counselor to have another child in hopes of bringing the spouses closer together? or divorced people who could not abide by a rigidly inhuman interpretation of the religious ban on artificial means of birth control that ignores the rights of conscience? Similar damage has been worked by well-intentioned healers as well. We are increasingly aware today of iatrogenetic sickness, that is, sickness caused by the healer or by the cure. (For example, medication for controlling hypertension can, if unsupervised, lead to gout.)

John Travis is a physician who is considerably less negative than Szasz in his judgment of religion. In fact, he admits that spiritual movements hold a concept of wellness similar to his. "But dissimilar," he says, "is their common tendency to elevate the leader of these practices to a demi-god position. I believe this weakens the message of self-responsibility."[5] However, the same could be said of the widespread popular view that "the physician is (like) God." In fact, the medical emphasis on "compliance" weakens the message of self-responsibility, too. Thus, both in religion and in medicine this danger is ever present, but giving in to it is not inevitable. In fact, such a posture is ordinarily eschewed by respectful and self-confident physicians and holy men/priests.

I believe, in fact, that it is possible not only to relate religion to wellness in a complete fashion that would embrace the totality of human life, but also to integrate religious practices and viewpoints into a distinctive wellness-promoting life-style. (For a successful effort that cuts across denominational lines, see the reference to the Greater Milwaukee Conference on Religion and Urban Affairs in the Resources list at the end of this book.) Certainly the time is right. To cite just one indication: A poll taken by George Gallup on January 20-23, 1978, showed that Americans' interest in spiritual life is growing. Approximately 19 percent of Americans are involved in Bible-study groups, with the young as involved as older persons. And Gallup projected that 6 percent, or some 9 million people, are involved in or experience inner or spiritual healing.

To these people as well as to other interested readers I hope to demonstrate now how any authentic spirituality, whether humanistic, Jewish, or Christian, can constitute an important element of a wellness life-style.

HUMANISTIC SPIRITUALITY

Humanistic spirituality is based on the common human experience that the human spirit yearns to know the truth, to pursue the best course of action, and to enjoy beauty. The spirit seeks to raise one's awareness and to increase one's sensitivity to the heights and riches of human spiritual achievement whether in art, music, drama, dance, literature, poetry, or any other way in which the human spirit expresses itself. The spirit also beckons the person to climb toward these heights. Indeed, each of these items has anagogical power, i.e., the ability to lead a person into higher realms of spiritual experience.

The popular Yiddish author Sholom Aleichem provides an illustration of this in his short story "The Fiddle." The boy in the story yearned to learn how to play the fiddle but never quite managed to arrange for that pleasure. One day he visited a retired Russian colonel named Tchetchek who volunteered to play for him. The boy was utterly swept away by the beauty of the music—a peak experience in pure humanistic spirituality.

People have such power too. The humanistic psychologist Sidney M. Jourard identified the spirit as the essential feature, the truly human aspect, of the person, and described its power thus:[6] Imagine a scale of 0 to 100. On this scale we can measure your spirit-titre, your level of spirituality. A normal reading would lie between 30 and 60. Sometimes, as in the fiddle story, you might hit higher, but it couldn't last for long; you'd have to come back down to earth again. If you fall below 30, you become ill and need someone to raise your spirit.

Now, there are some people among us who could be described as "inspiriting." These individuals have the power to raise the spirits of others to healing levels. We say such people have charisma or magnetism or something like that. Even if we don't have a name for it, we can recognize the reality.

The opposite of an inspiriting person is a "disinspiriting" person. The Yiddish language calls such individuals *yentas* or *kvetches*. These spoil-sports have the ability to demoralize others and lower their spirit level to the point where sickness can occur. Joe Btfisk in "L'il Abner" was a disinspiriting person. A black cloud followed him wherever he went. In his presence, hens couldn't lay, pianists couldn't play, and the sick became sicker.

I always insist that no one can do wellness to or for another. "You alone do it, but you don't do it alone."

To have a good level of wellness, you must surely have at least the average spirit-level. If you can sometimes move beyond that level, all the better for you. And if in addition you can become an inspiriting person, you can be a powerful force for motivating others to take greater control over their spiritual life.

Notice that humanistic spirituality does not call upon a deity or invoke religious beliefs. For those disinclined to be religious I am convinced that a humanistic approach to spirituality can work much the same wholesome effect. Devotees of Transcendental Meditation and similar movements would surely agree.

THE SPIRITUALITY OF JUDAISM

As the following development will show, the religion and spirituality of Judaism is life- and world-affirming to such a high degree that it can serve as an excellent basis for, indeed even as an integral element of, a wellness life-style. Those intellectually inclined will be able to discover much of value in Talmudic lore and rabbinical Judaism. Additional spiritual approaches can be developed aong the lines of neo-Hasidism—a movement familiar even to many non-Jews in the United States.

The Bible records the faith and religious practices of the ancient Jewish religion, but the Judaism which originated after the construction of the second Jewish Temple around 445/450 before the Common Era is the basic form of the Jewish religion that is practiced today. The faith and practices of Judaism are rooted in the Bible, but Judaism also draws on a vast treasury of materials other than the Bible.

The spirituality of Judaism is rooted in the Torah (the first five books of the Bible). In Genesis 2:7 we read that "the LORD God formed man out of the clay of the ground and blew into his nostrils the breath of life, and so man became a living being" (literally: "a living soul").

Two notions here relate to wellness: (1) It is the breath of God himself that is the source and permanence of human life; God is the ultimate meaning in life; (2) life is a gift from God, a share in God's own life, a treasure to be cherished, protected, nourished, and enhanced. The question of course is, how is this to be achieved?

The biblical conviction is that life is best promoted, pursued, and enhanced in obedience to the Torah, which points the way to fellowship with or closeness to God. God himself takes the initiative.

> The LORD, your God, will circumcise your hearts and the hearts of your descendants, that you may love the LORD, your God, with all your heart and all your soul, and so may live. (Deuteronomy 30:6)

In the Torah, God has revealed everything required for leading a full and enjoyable life. Some of the topics addressed therein sound rather mundane and trivial: e.g., baldness (Leviticus 13:40-44), foods to eat and to avoid (Leviticus 11), (hygiene in?) sexual intercourse (Leviticus 15:18). Yet, lest one be tempted to take them too lightly, there is a reminder to

> . . . carry out carefully every word of this *torah* [law]. For this is no trivial matter for you; rather, it means your very life, since it is by this means that you are to enjoy a long life on the land which you will cross the Jordan to occupy. (Deuteronomy 32:46-47)

By way of further encouragement, it is noted that the Torah is "something very near to you, already in your mouths and in your hearts; you have only to carry it out" (Deuteronomy 30:11-14).

This is similar to Travis's conviction that wellness means learning to uncover the solutions one already has. And in this light Leo Suenens unwittingly but most appropriately described the function of the wellness promoter when he said: "The greatest gift you can bestow upon another is not to share with him your riches, but rather to help him discover his own."

Indeed, what counts for wellness in the long run is self-determination, self-responsibility—the keystone of both biblical religion and modern-day wellness:

> I have set before you life and death, the blessing and the curse. Choose life, then, that you and your descendants may live, by loving the LORD, your God, heeding his voice, and holding fast to him. For that will mean life for you, a long life for you to live on the land which the LORD swore he would give to your father Abraham, Isaac, and Jacob. (Deuteronomy 30:19-20)

The entire goal and purpose of obeying the Torah is a long life, a full life, a satisfying life. The notion of a full life appears at least four times in the Jewish Scriptures when they describe the death of famous individuals:

> Then he [Abraham] breathed his last, dying at a ripe old age, grown old after a full life. . . . (Genesis 25:8)

> After a full life, he [Isaac] died as an old man. . . . (Genesis 35:29)

> He [David] died of a ripe old age, *rich in years* and wealth and glory. . . . (1 Chronicles 29:28)

> Then Job died, old and *full of years.* (Job 42:17)

In each instance the full life or fullness of years is expressed by a Hebrew phrase which essentially means "satisfied, sated, surfeited" with days (i.e., time). (The adjective also and more often applies to food and favor.) The English translators have generally rendered the phrase as "full life," capturing the Hebrew belief that a long life was a full life, a blessing, for it meant that one indeed had pleased God, lived in obedience to the Torah, and had achieved a closeness to God. In modern parlance we could say such a person had attained a high level of wellness—a purposeful and enjoyable life.

Two developments in Judaism can illustrate additional contributions that its contemporary spirituality can make to a wellness life-style: rabbinism, and Polish hasidism. Rabbinism is that aspect of Judaism established by the scribes and Pharisees and then developed by their successors, the rabbis. In essence, it focused on the oral legal tradition that was given to Moses on Mount Sinai together with the written Torah but that was first collected in the Mishnah (about 180 of the Common Era) and later repeated with commentary (the Gemara) in the Talmud, both in Palestine and in Babylonia in the fifth and sixth centuries, respectively. It is the Babylonian Talmud that has been the focal point of rabbinical study even to this day.

The Talmud ranges over the entire realm of human life, but in the beginning the rabbis were especially concerned with helping people understand the proper observance of the Torah so that they would be able to walk in a path pleasing to God. (The Hebrew word for this legal discussion is *halakah*, from the verb *hlk* meaning "to walk.") The aim was twofold: to insure the proper observance of God's laws, and to dispel anxiety from Jews who wanted to be as perfectly obedient as possible. Thus, to guide the pious Jew who wanted to know exactly when to recite the obligatory *Shema*, there is a lengthy discussion of exactly what—visually—constitutes sunset and sunrise (colors of the rays, sky, etc.).

Later the Talmud incorporated many non-legal subjects: theology, history, ethics, lives of the sages, legends, and folklore. Here is one example of Talmudic advice that encourages a wellness life-style:

> Rab Beroka of Be Hozae was often in the Market at Be Lapat. There he would meet [the Prophet] Elijah. Once he said to Elijah: Is there anyone in this market who shall have the world to come? Elijah said to him: No. They were standing there when two men came along. Elijah said to him: These shall have the world to come. Rab Beroka went to them and said: What is your occupation? They said to him: We are jesters, and make the sad to laugh. When we see two men quarreling, we strive hard to make peace between them. (Ta'anit, 22a)

Outside the Talmud there are other anecdotes that add further considerations to the establishment of a Jewish high-level wellness life-style. Here is a story about Hillel that illustrates what we might call a consideration of primary prevention that could certainly pertain also to wellness:

> When he had finished the lesson with his pupils, he accompanied them part of the way. They said to him: "Master, where are you going?" "To perform a religious duty." "Which religious duty?" "To bathe in the bath house." "Is that a religious duty?" He answered them: "If somebody is appointed to scrape and clean the statues of the king that are set up in the theaters and circuses, is paid to do the work, and furthermore associates with the nobility, how much more so should I, who am created in the divine image and likeness, take care of my body!" (Leviticus Rabbah, 34:3)

Bathing is certainly a good health practice. To do it so as to avoid disease is a good health observance. But to do it with motivation similar to Hillel's is to make it also a wellness practice.

Furthermore, Jews realize that ill health blunts spiritual sensitivity, and since this sensitivity is a prized value among observant Jews, they make every effort to avoid sickness, maintain good health, and promote even better health.

It should also be noted that in Judaism, study of and practice of the Torah are inseparable, because the Torah is a concrete way of salvation. "Studying the Torah and applying it to life," says Kurt Hruby, noted Jewish scholar, "are works of sanctification and are at the same time salvation and the permanent accomplishment of the main task that God has confided to his people."[7] The importance given to study in Judaism is similar to the conviction of wellness enthusiasts that wellness depends very much on reading and studying about a wide range of subjects. "Much of wellness education," writes Travis, "involves verbal skills, psychological awareness and developed intellectual capabilities."[8] He concludes from this that wellness is not generally attainable by the poor. Their concerns (e.g., food, shelter, and job) are such that though they are basic to wellness, the concerns are so persistent that the poor may never be free to seek higher levels of wellness. (But see page 43.)

Curiously, the rabbinic discussions of the Torah as recorded in the Talmud and as discussed and practiced after the Talmudic period had a similar effect upon the common, unlettered or less literate Jew. How could such a person strive for the full life: a satisfying life, a high level of Jewish wellness?

A spiritual reaction arose to counter the over-formalistic attitude toward the prescriptions of the Torah. It passed through several stages, including a mystical

and esoteric phase, until it reached (about the eleventh
century) the first real pietistic trend in Judaism: German
Hasidism.

German Hasidism was a dour form of piety with an
emphasis on ethics and insistence on purity of intention,
deep faith, and permanent communion with God in
prayer. It remained austere even when it spread to
Poland. But in the eighteenth century an unbridgeable
gap opened between the pious scholars of Hasidism and
the great mass of the people, who were then
experiencing serious political and economic problems.
At this time there appeared Rabbi Israel ben Eliezer
(1700-1760), better known as the Ba'al *Shem Tov* (*Besht*,
for short—an acronym), who took pity on his people's
wretchedness and decided to bring them a message of
liberation. Though lacking in Talmudic learning, Besht
nevertheless successfully taught that one should serve
God in joy, taking strength in the knowledge that the
whole universe is filled with the glory of God. The only
way to approach God, according to Besht, is the way of
fervor and joyful service. Moreover, one does not have
to be a scholar or an initiate to accomplish this service.
Every person, no matter what his or her station or
ability, could thus achieve the full and happy life that
results from pleasing God.

Besht developed a wellness-promoting life-style, if
we may retroject a contemporary notion, for the man in
the street. He opened spiritual horizons for such a
person that were unthinkable before this time. Two key
elements in Besht's program were prayer and positive
judgment. He viewed prayer as an intensely personal
relationship with God. Better to pray spontaneously and
fervently than at fixed hours and in fixed formulas.
Such a prayer, taught Besht, removed a person from all
preoccupations and allowed him or her to live a new
kind of life. (Think of Tevye in *Fiddler on the Roof*, who
yearns for a seat in the synagogue by the eastern wall
where he could pray to his heart's delight.)

Positive judgment was a principle drawn from the *Pirqe Abot*, the *Sayings of the Fathers* (1:6): "Judge all men charitably," i.e., positively, always giving the benefit of the doubt to everyone. He who practiced both these principles became a *ṣaddiq*, a just man, a leader for others. Hasidism was all but wiped out during the war (1939-1945) but was given a new lease on life in the writings of Martin Buber and more recently those of Elie Wiesel and was reincarnated as neo-Hasidism in various communities under the aegis of rabbis from the communities of Lubavitch, Szatmar, Bobov and others.

These are but a few of the riches in the Judaic tradition that can serve as the basis for a high-level wellness life-style.

CHRISTIAN SPIRITUALITY

Christian spirituality is basically one: It is a development of the human spirit rooted in Christ, his life and his teachings. But Christian spirituality is not like mass-produced, ready-to-wear T-shirts which differ one from another only in size. No, Christian spirituality is rather a patterning of one's life after the quality and direction of the life of Jesus, a patterning which is self-designed and to a great extent developed according to one's preferences and interpretations. From this perspective, Christian spirituality is like Travis's view of wellness: It is created and directed by the individual or group. This explains the diversity of Christian spiritualities: Augustinian, Benedictine, Dominican, Franciscan, Lutheran, Methodist, Ignatian, and so on.

The basic source of Christian spirituality is the Christian Scriptures, for this is where we can learn about Jesus and how to lead a life in imitation of his. But even though they are inspired and inerrant, the Christian Scriptures are incomplete and imperfectly developed. Much more happened than has been recorded. Jesus is presented in the gospels from a variety of viewpoints and therefore is cast in a multiplicity of images.

The Synoptic Gospels (Matthew, Mark, Luke) generally propose what might be described as an ascetic spirituality. The Greek root of the word *ascetic, askein,* means "to exercise." Ascetic spirituality is one that promotes closeness to or union with God through a certain set of exercises: self-denial which can be practiced through vigilance and prayer (Mark 14:38). Self-denial actually has two dimensions: negative, or world-denying, and positive, or world-affirming.

The negative, or world-denying, dimension of self-denial involves three steps: renunciation, as in Matthew 19:21, which suggests selling all, giving the proceeds to the poor, and following Jesus (a detachment from materialistic values); a certain distance from persons, as in Matthew 10:37 and Luke 14:25-26, which say that anyone so attached to others that he or she can't be free to seek Jesus is unworthy of him; and finally, the actual process of taking up one's cross, accepting the daily reversals of life, and following Jesus, as in Matthew 16:24, Mark 8:34, and Luke 9:23, which say that he who thinks he's lost something will actually gain that and much more.

The positive, or world-affirming, dimension of self-denial is love of neighbor and love of God joined to the lessening of destructive self-seeking and of unproductive self-indulgence proclaimed in today's "I gotta be me" (see Matthew 22:37-40 and Mark 12:30-31).

This kind of ascetical spirituality appears to be a prelude to wellness life-style. (Indeed, in classical spirituality it is identified as the basic or purgative way.) Travis prefers to work with people who have already begun to put their lives in order by reducing if not entirely removing from their life-style the popular American health-defeating practices, like the alcohol-dominated "attitude-adjustment hour." A high-level wellness spirituality would analogously require that the spiritually minded person should have done likewise in his or her spiritual life.

The Gospel of John differs from this rather austere picture painted by the Synoptics. John describes a mystical form of spirituality, i.e., a development of the human spirit as a result of a higher level of life in union with God through the mystery of his grace. John invites the individual to allow himself or herself to be reborn (3:5), to become engrafted to the vine that is Jesus (15), to let divine life enter and flow through one's person (14:23), to take one's share in a new life, life to the full (10:10).

Paul the Apostle combines the ascetical and the mystical elements in his life, at least according to what we can deduce from his letters. He explicitly admits that Christ is at the core of his life:

> For, to me, 'life' means Christ. (Philippians 1:21)

> It was through the Torah that I died to the Torah, to live for God. I have been crucified with Christ, and the life I live now is not my own; Christ is living in me. I still live my human life, but it is a life of faith in the Son of God, who loved me and gave himself for me. (Galatians 2:19-20; my translation in part).

> If anyone is in Christ, he is a new creation. (2 Corinthians 5:17)

These texts identify the mystical element in Paul's spirituality. The phrase "in Christ," which appears some 165 times in Paul's letters, identifies the close union of Christ and the Christian and even connotes a symbiotic relationship between them. The phrase "Christ [is living]

in me" (Galatians 2:20, 2 Corinthians 13:5; Romans
8:10; Colossians 1:27; Ephesians 3:17) connotes a
dynamic influence of Christ on the Christian who is
incorporated into him. This same idea is reflected in
Paul's discussion of Christians as members of the Body
of Christ. A thorough review of Paul's letters with a
sensitivity to this aspect uncovers many elements of this
mystical dimension of spirituality that can contribute to
the formation of a high-level Christian wellness life-style.
(Those who think this sounds rather self-abnegating
need only recall Sholom Aleichem's description of the
boy's reaction to the Colonel's music.)

Yet there is also an ascetic, combative dimension to
Paul's spirituality. He borrows vocabulary from sport
and describes himself as having run the good race,
fought the good fight. In turn he reminds his readers to
do likewise.

> You must lay aside your former way of life and the
> old self which deteriorates through illusion and
> desire, and acquire a fresh, spiritual way of
> thinking. You must put on that new man created
> in God's image, whose justice and holiness are born
> of truth. (Ephesians 4:22-24)

He follows these verses with a list of concrete practices
in which one might "exercise" in order to reach a higher
level of spirituality, a greater degree of spiritual wellness.

In sum, both the ascetical and the mystical
approaches to spirituality as recorded in the Christian
Scriptures lend themselves to the formation of a
distinctive Christian approach to high-level wellness,
pleasurable and purposeful living.

The history of post-biblical Christian spirituality
records an evolutionary development through
anthropocentric, theocentric, and Christocentric phases
(prompted mainly by the historical period). Francis of

Assisi, the thirteenth-century religious figure who firmly established and developed the Christocentric phase, is particularly fitting as an inspiration for any Christian who would want to begin to define and develop a Christian high-level wellness spirituality.

Francis recognized no spiritual masters (which answers Travis's fear that spiritual leaders tend to assume a demigod position at some point in time), and he depended on no other school of spirituality. Francis's insistence that "no one showed me . . . but the Most High Himself" is without doubt a straightforward statement of self-direction if there ever was one. His biography is an exciting story of his steady insistence on his own way and of his unswerving resolve not to allow anything alien to be imposed on him and his vision. Francis extended this same freedom to his followers. He would impose nothing on them, so long as they in turn would impose nothing on him.

Yet Franciscan spirituality does draw from common sources. For Francis and all his followers the Christian Scriptures were the basic source of life-style: the gospel, only the gospel, and the entire gospel—understood with concrete practicality and applied to life with unhesitating immediacy. No other Christian spirituality before or after his has taken such a comprehensive view of Christian Scriptures, of the life-style of Jesus. And Francis learned this especially in the liturgy, whose annual cycles nourished his piety, fed his yearnings, and inspired him with new insights for his ever-expanding experience of life.

The followers of Francis obviously looked also to Francis himself for inspiration: his attitudes, outlooks, preferences, his very own life-style. And the intriguing result has been more than a seven-and-half-century following of men and women in an amazing variation on this basic vision: the Friars Minor, the Conventuals, the Capuchins, the Poor Clares, the Colettines, the Third Order Regular, the Third Order Secular, and countless unattached and unofficial devotees of the Poor Man of Assisi.

Franciscan spirituality, in fact, may be one way of doing what Travis believes to be nearly impossible: conducting an authentic pursuit of wellness available to and effectively operative for the poor. Francis and his followers have through the centuries freely chosen to travel this lesser path, this way of minority, and have managed to do it in a fascinating variety of satisfying ways. Other Christian spiritualities can undoubtedly offer still other paths to high-level wellness, but Franciscanism nevertheless has perennial popularity. The richness of the Christian tradition has something for everyone.

CONCLUSION

A final note must be added about the spirituality of both Judaism and Christianity. The Targumic scholar Roger Le Déaut has noted: "The position occupied by the Pasch in Jewish and Christian spirituality needs treatment in great depth, since 'Christian spirituality and Jewish spirituality are both paschal in principle.' "[9]

The word *paschal* identifies and describes a movement from bondage to freedom (as in the Exodus) as well as a passage from death to life (as in the death and resurrection of Jesus). The two notions are relatively interchangeable: Jews can accept the Pasch as a passage from death to life, as when they speak of the Holocaust (which must never happen again) as a contributing factor to the establishment of the modern state of Israel. And the death and resurrection of Christ can also be understood as a movement from the bondage of sin and Satan to the freedom of the children of God.

This basic paschal principle should perhaps constitute the cornerstone of a wellness life-style based either on Jewish or Christian spirituality. Wellness, as we have been describing it, can give the impression of being utopian or polyannish. That is far from the truth, and the Pasch can prevent such an erroneous understanding from creeping into a wellness life-style.

Some Christians have expressed an understanding of the Pasch in the phrase "*After* death, life." Since life is unfair and full of setbacks, failures, and disappointments, Christians offered it up, suffered, stuck it out, believing that true purposeful life and pleasure would begin after death, after each person's resurrection. A careful re-reading of the Christian sources shows that interpretation to be mistaken. Pasch is best expressed in the phrase "*Out of* death, life." Out of daily deaths, ascetical deaths, and other kinds of demises, one springs to new life, to higher levels of life, to full life. This principle reveals yet another reason why health and wellness are not identical.

Every spirituality is the fruit of a slow and progressive elaboration by persons (and sometimes generations of individuals) who in the life of a community have labored in the same direction, in the steps of a founder, contributing their own experience and doctrine to the fundamental experience of the founder.

The establishment and development of a high-level wellness spirituality would probably follow the three stages of development characteristic of other spiritualities:

1. The period of the founder and immediate disciples.

2. The period of theological justification.

3. The period of development through the centuries.

It is difficult to identify the founder and immediate disciples of a high-level wellness spirituality. Audiences

have variously noted that these ideas remind them of
Paul Tournier, Josef Goldbrunner, Ira Progoff, and many
others.

We are perhaps now in the period of justification,
attempting to answer such questions as these: Does
wellness have all the elements required for recognition
as a spirituality? Can wellness genuinely be understood
as a form of religiously based spirituality? I believe that
this chapter makes a significant contribution, at least as
a beginning, to that justification.

The period of development is also already under
way.[10] Perhaps it must move hand in glove with
justification. The very nature of wellness demands that
each person develop it according to a personal vision.
As my rabbinical teachers always reminded me: "Where
there are two rabbis, there are three opinions." How
stifling for Christians to have thought for so long that
where there are millions of Christians, there must be
one and only one opinion! This was a gross
misunderstanding of tradition, for even the Scriptures
do not support it. Christians have always had the
freedom (if not the encouragement) to be as unique as
Francis was, and as he encouraged his followers to be.
The next chapter will help you look for that uniqueness.

NOTES

1. Karl Rahner and Herbert Vorgrimler, *Theological Dictionary*, ed. Cornelius Ernst (New York: Herder & Herder, 1965), p. 445. See the articles on "Spirit," pp. 444-45 and on "Sensuality," p. 432, where the authors note: "The derogatory sense of sensuality which is now its usual one has its justification, but it is worth trying to revive the first and more original sense of the word." And that in 1961 in the German original edition!

2. Additional information about Meadowlark and similar programs can be found in Donald Ardell, *High Level Wellness: An Alternative to Doctors, Drugs, and Disease* (Emmaus, Pa.: Rodale Press, 1978).

3. Thomas S. Szasz, *The Myth of Mental Illness: Foundations of a Theory of Personal Conduct* (New York: Harper & Row, p. 192; a revised edition appeared in 1974). I hold Dr. Szasz in very high regard in the field of medicine and psychiatry. He is a peerless leader and internationally respected spokesman in the field of mental health. In religious and biblical matters, however, his comments appear to reflect the knowledge of the common person in the street, since I am aware of no sacred text, commentary, or scientific publication that would support Szasz's understanding and interpretation.

4. For example, Szasz in *Myth*, p. 196, cites Matthew 5:3: "Blessed are the poor in spirit: for theirs is the kingdom of heaven." Then he interprets: "Man should be 'poor in spirit'—i.e., stupid, submissive: Do not be smart, well-informed, or assertive." With his interpretation, Szasz concludes that the beatitudes (Matthew 5:1-12) are "probably the best-known illustration of the rules fostering dependency and disability." The reader is encouraged to read Szasz in his entirety, for a position that contradicts and denies the thrust of this book. As a biblical scholar, I respect his positions but could write another book to show that he has misused or misinterpreted the sacred texts. Moreover, as a believer who lives the Scriptures as well as his education (elementary, secondary, graduate, and postgraduate) has taught him, I can only say that my life-experience based on the beatitudes is not what Szasz portrays. In fact, I have still to meet someone who lives by the Christian gospel and yet looks like what Szasz describes. Perhaps my experience is still limited. Nevertheless, I would further invite the readers to seek out books written about the beatitudes and decide for themselves how

well Szasz has understood and interpreted them. The unpublished class notes of Dr. Bruce Malina, "New Testament Morality" (Omaha: The Creighton University, 1969), pp. 57-108, are representative of how the beatitudes are taught to college undergraduates in Catholic colleges across the country. Read and enjoy.

5. Travis, *Wellness Workbook*, section for health professionals, p. 5.

6. Sidney M. Jourard, *The Transparent Self*, rev. ed. (New York: D. Van Nostrand Co., 1971), pp. 73-100.

7. Roger LeDéaut, Annie Jaubert and Kurt Hruby, *The Spirituality of Judaism* (St. Meinrad, Indiana: Abbey Press, 1977), p. 63, in the section authored by Hruby. This book translates an article that appeared in the *Dictionnaire de Spiritualite*, an outstanding source on spirituality for those who read French.

8. Travis, *Wellness Workbook*, section for health professionals, p. 45. I think the key word in the conclusion Travis draws is *generally.* In addition, this position reflects Travis's thinking in 1977 when he wrote that section of his book. He may have changed his opinion, just as I have come to realize that poverty is really no barrier to wellness.

9. LeDéaut, *Spirituality*, p. 32, quoting A. Neher, *Moise et la vocation juive* (Paris, 1956), p. 127.

10. Richard P. McBrien's *Catholicism* (Minneapolis: Winston Press, 1980), Chapter XVIII, pp. 1057-99, presents a synthetic overview of past and present in Catholic-Christian spirituality. My most recent attempt to develop a high-level wellness Catholic-Christian spirituality with Franciscan flavor is *"Developing an Holistic Spirituality"* (Sewanee, Tenn.: The University of the South, 1980). This latter program develops the ideas of this chapter at greater length (approximately ninety pages). A sketch of how this spirituality can serve as a leaven in a worshiping community such as a Catholic parish is presented in the audio-cassette program *Parish Wellness* (Kansas City, Mo.: NCR Cassettes, 1980). The original, live presentation of this chapter's content can be heard on the audio-cassette *Spirituality and High Level Wellness,* (Kansas City, Mo.: NCR Cassettes, 1978).

CHAPTER THREE

WELLNESS AND LIFE'S PURPOSE

Testing for wellness as defined in this book means at least two things: defining your purpose in life, and determining the measure of your self-responsibility and self-determination. The basic questions are:

- Do you have a purpose in life?
- To what extent have you freely determined your purpose in life?
- Do you continue to bear responsibility for your decisions?

The answers to these simple questions can be surprising. For the most part, purpose in life has been assigned to us: by the culture; by the family, which largely reinforces culture; or by religion, which sometimes contradicts culture though more often than not supports it.

In our culture, for instance, the proper thing to do is get an education, mainly for the purpose of getting a job, so that you can finally attain financial

independence and security and then live happily ever
after. This has become true for women as well as for
men, though many women are still expected to accept
the role of wife and mother rather than to pursue a
career.

These purposes in American life are so universally
and unquestioningly accepted that anyone who selects a
different option does so only with great difficulty and at
the risk of being chided or ridiculed. A woman who
chooses to delay marriage to pursue a career will be
warned not to delay too long lest she become an old
maid. A man who chooses to study the liberal or fine
arts will be reminded that he will have difficulty finding
a job and earning a living after graduation. It is a rare
student who pursues an educational program for any
value other than the generally sex-linked roles
determined by society. Freedom for self-determination
does exist, but it is quite restricted.

American families reinforce the pattern. The
traditional authoritarian family pattern still prevails in
the United States and still insists that children should
become something that makes the parents happy. "My
daughter, the doctor" brings more joy to a family than
"my son, the ballet dancer," though "my daughter,
mother of my grandchildren" is still the most satisfying
phrase of the three.[1]

Religion too has contributed its share to affirming
the pattern. "God made me to know him, love him, and
serve him faithfully on earth, so that I might be happy
with him forever in heaven," said the old penny
catechism. Serving God faithfully on earth is frequently
interpreted to mean doing what society proclaims is
proper and correct. The Northern European Protestant
tradition, for instance, believed that all work is
meaningful; therefore all people should work. This
tradition furnished its pioneer American descendants

with a work ethic which has been a cornerstone of
American society throughout its history.

But some people, such as the born-wealthy and
those on welfare, never work, and yet they seem better
off than those who do. Others get a good education but
can't seem to get the job that should follow—e.g.,
women or teachers and lawyers in a market glutted with
their skills. Less qualified candidates for a position are
frequently hired in preference to more qualified ones.
And society has even adopted the phrase "over-
qualified" as a euphemism for "not dumb enough" in
the sense of "potential trouble maker." Life is unfair and
becomes more so with each passing day.

Southern European Catholics devised a solution to
the unfairness of life which they experienced in
meaningless work situations. They allotted time in each
day for siesta and filled the year with religious fiestas.
They balanced periods of boring or meaningless work
with periods of wholesome recreation and activities that
reminded them of life's true purpose and meaning.

As the leisure of some gradually became the
livelihood of others, this solution lost its appeal. Today
the overriding purpose in American life seems simply to
earn money (make a living) whether the job is
meaningful or not. As the old saying goes: No mon, no
fun, my son. Our freedom for determining a distinctive
purpose in life is more restricted than we realize.

I believe that high levels of wellness, that is,
genuinely satisfying goals and purposes in life, are still
possible and available to anyone willing to recapture the
eroded power of self-determination and to accept full
responsibility for life-decisions. I further believe that
spirituality and/or religion constitute key elements in
measuring present levels of wellness and in changing
them if necessary, or in setting even higher goals in
wellness.

Religion and spirituality sometimes contradict the

goals and purposes in life proposed by culture. I believe that a fresh consideration of humanistic, Jewish, and Christian beliefs, spiritualities, and values can clarify our puzzlements, explain our frustrations and disappointments, and suggest new ways to redefine a satisfying life style that can be personally designed, freely pursued, and highly fulfilling.

HUMANISTIC REFLECTIONS ON WELLNESS

Wellness educators who espouse humanistic values use a variety of tests and inventories to help persons examine the meaning those persons give to life and to encourage them to state their life's purposes and goals clearly and explicitly. Two of the more popular tests are the Wellness Inventory and the Purpose in Life Test.

The Wellness Inventory was designed and copyrighted by John Travis, M.D.[2] It is a ninety-nine-question test keyed to fourteen basic paperback books which teach self-responsibility in many areas of living. The questions cover ten specific areas:

1. productivity, relaxation, sleep;
2. personal care and safety;
3. nutritional awareness;
4. environmental awareness;
5. physical activity;
6. expression of emotions and feelings;
7. community involvement;
8. creativity, self-expression;
9. automobile safety;
10. parenting.

There are a handful of "footnotes" to the eight-page test explaining some of the questions whose significance may be less than obvious.

The Inventory is not a once-for-always, right-or-wrong kind of test but a tool for self-exploration to identify areas of life-style that might require special attention. For instance, a low score in expression of emotions and feeling might suggest that you need to seek help for improvement in that area, or need to reconsider that aspect of your life-style. Inhibited emotions and unexpressed feelings can do serious damage to physical, emotional, social, and spiritual health. They can also make life more miserable than pleasurable. This is why wellness educators insist that each person needs at least four hugs a day to maintain a good level of wellness!

The Inventory is particularly good for expanding your awareness of aspects of living often overlooked or taken for granted. But it seems to believe that knowledge is virtue, that knowing it means you'll do it. It doesn't directly address the question of motivation. Why should you be concerned about a poor score in any area? Why try to do something about it?

Some answers to these questions can be discovered in the three-part Purpose in Life Test designed by James C. Crumbaugh, Ph. D., and Leonard T. Maholick, M.D.[3] Part One uses a scale of one to seven to measure feelings about life, goals, the world, free choice, and related concepts. Part Two lists thirteen phrases to be completed in sentences. For instance, "The whole purpose of my life. . . ." The final part of the test asks you to write a paragraph describing in detail your aims, ambitions, goals, and so on.

The test provides an opportunity to reflect very pointedly and directly on your answers to life's meaning, purpose, goals, and satisfactions. In combination with the Inventory this test can show you not only what your level of wellness is but why your level is high or low. For instance, the Inventory can highlight health-destructive practices in your daily life, such as smoking two or more packages of cigarettes. You can, of course, easily shrug them off with comments such as "Oh well, that's life;" or "We all have to die from something, so why not from lung cancer?"

The problem is that most Americans don't believe such a thing as cancer can happen to them. And if it does, they have such faith in medical science that they believe that when it does, science will have a cure: lung transplants, non-cancer-causing cigarettes, and so on.

The Purpose in Life Test, however, can point out that you have no purpose in life, or that the purpose assigned by culture, family, or religion makes no sense to you. So your heavy smoking habit could be an attempt to cope with a senseless or aggravating job; it could also be an unconscious attempt to shorten a meaningless life.

The next move is up to you. No one can do wellness for you. It is by definition self-designed and personally implemented. If you are indeed smoking excessively as a means of coping with an intolerable job or family situation, is there anything you can do? Are you still free to determine your life? One way to find out is by means of a simple value-clarification exercise.[4]

We believe that we have freely chosen our values. Pause for a moment and list the significant and normative values in your life. Then recall the nature of a value. It is something freely chosen from alternatives with full knowledge of the consequences and then acted upon. It is something you cherish, prize, and celebrate. You publicly affirm it when asked or challenged, and you integrate it into your regular life-style.

The following chart lists seven indicators of a value. Record your value in the space above each column and then put a check mark by each indicator that is true of your value. Use your job, occupation, or profession as an example.

1. Free choice;					
2. from alternatives;					
3. full knowledge of consequences;					
4. cherish/prize the choice;					
5. affirm it publicly;					
6. do it;					
7. repeat it as a life-style.					

Work is unquestionably a part of the goal and purpose of American life.[5] Our society reminds all of us from youth that no one gets or should get anything for nothing; that everyone should work for a living; that everyone also has the freedom to select a specific job, occupation, or profession.

Beginning with the first value indicator, was it a free choice for you to begin work, or would you rather loaf, be an eternal student, or go on welfare? Did you know the alternatives to work or to this job? And did you know all the consequences of working and loafing? For instance, did you freely choose to begin work when you really wanted to spend ten years studying to be a physician? Will you continue to work as an important part of your life-style?

Do the same with your specific job or profession. Did you freely choose to be a veterinarian, e.g., or did you go to vet school because you weren't accepted by an medical school? (A study published in a medical journal indicated that the most popular second choice for those not accepted into medical school is vet school. What does that suggest about purpose in life: helping people? or making a living?)

Few persons mark their values as "free choice." They may freely choose to repeat them as part of their life-style, but they frequently didn't choose the value freely at the outset. Five check marks constitute a value indicator; the given item might well be a value for you. Seven check marks indicate a belief strong enough to form part of your purpose in life.

Consider the case of Giovanni Bernardone, known to history as Francis of Assisi. He was the son of a cloth merchant and knew financial comfort. He also chose to experience poverty. Having done that, he selected poverty as his way of life. It was a choice, freely made, from alternatives, and with full knowledge of the consequences.

Mark well that Francis was not a beggar. He worked, and he demanded that his followers work. He believed in work but not in profit. Only when there was no work would he allow himself or others to count on the charity of others. When he was paid he shared with the poor.

Francis was happy with his choice, cherished it, and affirmed it publicly. When he decided to espouse poverty as a value, he summoned his father to the town square and in the presence of bishop and townsfolk stripped himself naked, returned all to his father, and said henceforth God would be his father.

Later in life he wrote poems and songs in honor of Lady Poverty, as he termed this key value of his life-style. He acted on his choice and lived it until the day he died. The same can be said of Albert Schweitzer and many others. But the same can also be said of those who smoke tobacco to excess or drink alcoholic beverages to excess. The fact is, value clarification simply examines the process of self-determination and measures the degree of freedom in the process of forming your life-style and setting your life's goals and purposes. It doesn't tell you whether your values are good or bad, right or wrong.

The relationship of your values to your purpose in

life can run two ways. If freedom for creative expression is the most important value in your life, chances are that your goal and purpose in life will be to create something for humanity to appreciate, and to be recognized for your contribution. You might even like to earn a living in this way, but it is unlikely that you expect to become a millionaire. In fact, you might even be willing to live in poverty just to retain the joy and satisfaction of continuing to create freely.

On the other hand, if your goal and purpose in life is to become a millionaire, money and ways to get it will be high among your values. You might even adopt the motto of the hedonist outlaw: "Get rich, live fast, die young, make a handsome corpse, and leave a widow in comfort." Either relationship is possible; the choice is up to you.

Humanistic wellness educators believe that life is worth living, that human life is the highest value, and that each person should freely choose to live it any way he or she desires. Each wellness educator espouses some framework, whether existentialism, personalism, materialism, or spiritualism, but leaves the individual the option of choosing whatever framework pleases him or her. The content of your purpose in life as well as your values will differ accordingly.

A JEWISH TEST FOR WELLNESS

"Choose life!" Moses urged the Jews shortly before he died (Deuteronomy 30:19). Throughout their history they did. But life's circumstances frequently raised questions about the purpose and meaning of life and about why life should be preferred to anything else. No one asked the questions more thoroughly or more pointedly than Qoheleth, a wise Jew who lived during the third century before the Common Era. Notice especially what he and the rest of Jewish tradition say about "work" in life.

The book recording his reflections is found in the third part of the Jewish Scriptures, known as the *Kethubim* or the Writings. The opening sentence: "The words of Qoheleth ben David, king in Jerusalem" is also the title of the book in the Hebrew Bible, but it is referred to by its brief title, Qoheleth. (Non-Jewish bibles often call this book Ecclesiastes, from the Greek translation of the word Qoheleth.)

Qoheleth is not so much a name as a title: It refers to one who holds the office of speaker (preacher, teacher) of the assembly (in Hebrew the assembly is the *qahal*; hence the name). Qoheleth was quite knowledgeable about life and widely experienced in the ways and workings of the world. He wrote down for posterity what he shared in the assembly.

He says he spent his entire life searching and investigating all things that are done under the sun (1:13). His book records his conclusions about the meaning and purpose in life. The report is divided into two sections: First, Qoheleth presents the result of his thorough investigation of life's purposes, meanings, and values (1:12—6:9); then he presents his conclusions drawn from the investigations (6:10—11:6).[6]

Qoheleth set out to "understand what is best for men to do under the heavens during the limited days of their life" (2:3). Methodically and comprehensively he personally tested—in his own experience as well as in discussion and reading—meanings and purposes in life to see where they might lead.

With customary Semitic concreteness he began with a study of pleasure-seeking. He amassed slaves, property, cattle, gold, silver, and denied himself no pleasure. But in the end, he noted that all these could pass and that his efforts were thus useless, vanity, and a chase after wind. (This phrase is Qoheleth's common conclusion in this section. It also serves as a literary divider between topics.)

Next he considered wisdom and folly (2:12-17). Of
course, he preferred learning and wisdom to foolishness
and stupidity. But as a matter of fact, both the wise
man and the fool die. Neither is remembered or
commemorated. So why be intelligent? This too is
vanity and a chase after wind.

Then in a series of four meditations he turned his
attention to work and the results of toil (2:18—6:9). First
(2:18-26), he pointed out what everyone knows: You
can't take it with you. He struggled to gain wisdom and
become a good teacher, but there's no telling whether a
wise man or a fool will come after to take his place. No
one knows what kind of heir will follow. What a
frustration, what a chase after wind!

His second consideration (3:1—4:6), which includes
the famous poem on the appointed time for everything,
shows that a person can never seem to hit upon the
right time to act. God has appointed a proper time to
everything, but he has put timelessness into the human
heart. This is precisely what confuses a person about the
right time for action, and what makes human work
fruitless and chancy. You pay your money, and you take
your chances.

Moreover, the world is not just; or as the moderns
say, life is unfair. Since there is a proper time for
everything, there must also be a proper judgment for
everything. But people and beasts all suffer the same
fate, both in life and after death. In fact, Qoheleth notes
that the only ones luckier than those presently alive
who know life's injustices are those yet unborn because
they don't see anything at all.

And what about competition and rivalry that seem
to pervade all work? Well, Qoheleth does not suggest
laziness or outright refusal to work, but on the other
hand he does not encourage overexertion or
workaholism. He simply points out his difficulty with
the traditional teaching on diligence: It appears to lead

inexorably to rivalry. And then work becomes nothing but a chase after wind.

Qoheleth's third reflection on the fruits of work (4:7-16) is about the "second one." It is good to have a "second," a companion, an assistant, an heir, because "two are better than one." But on the other hand, the "second"—as he illustrates in a story of an old king—may actually set out to obliterate your place in history. This too is a vanity.

His final meditation on work's rewards (4:17—6:9) points out that even if you lose sleep over your wealth, you can still lose everything in many unexpected ways. Qoheleth has only one pertinent piece of advice, which he offers now (5:12-19) as he has three times earlier (2:24; 3:13; and 3:22): Enjoy life, enjoy the fruits of your work, stop worrying—it doesn't help. This is the balance to his repeated observation that everything is vanity and a chase after wind.

As he closes this first section, he elaborates a little on his "enjoy life" theme (6:1-9). He has previously repeated that enjoying life and the fruits of work is a gift of God. But sometimes God does not give you an opportunity to enjoy the rewards of your labor, and some persons have an insatiable appetite for enjoyment and let their desires wander beyond the present. The simple advice is: Enjoy it now as life offers the opportunity.

In the second section of his book (6:10—11:6), where he presents the conclusion he has drawn from his investigations, Qoheleth notes that we simply do not know or understand what God has done. As a consequence, (1) we cannot determine a proper course of action (6:10—8:17), and (2) we do not know the future (9:1—11:6). (The phrases serving as literary dividers in these sections are "not find out/who can find out" and "do not know/no knowledge.")

Qoheleth's discussion of our inability to discover

the right and proper things to do (especially in chapters 7 and 8) is a criticism of traditional wisdom. The accepted views taught that suffering is to some extent advantageous; justice is rewarded and wickedness is punished; women are worse than men when it comes to folly and evildoing; and sages and kings are to be respected and obeyed.

In four sections, Qoheleths objects to each view. First (7:1-14) he cites the traditional proverbs on the value of adversity and suffering but shows that wise men can be corrupted while suffering adversity.

Next (7:15-24) he points out what nearly all human experience verifies: The wicked prosper, the just suffer, and no one can understand retribution as we see it in this life.

As for women being more foolish and evil than men (7:25-29), Qoheleth says that he found men to be scarcely better than women. His empirical evidence showed that among a thousand women, he could find not a single wise one; but out of a thousand men, he found only one!

Finally (8:1-17), while the sage and king are presumed to be knowledgeable and worthy of respect and obedience, it is clear that the sage doesn't know some very basic answers about the future and that the king is as powerless as anybody else in regard to putting off death or prolonging life.

In his reflections on the fact that we don't know what the future holds in store (9:1—11:6), Qoheleth repeats many ideas previously mentioned and reminds his readers that life is precious in itself: "A live dog is better off than a dead lion" (9:4)—and advises them to enjoy the present moment:

> Go, eat your bread with joy and drink your wine with a merry heart, because it is now that God favors your works. . . . Enjoy life with the wife

whom you love, all the days of the fleeting life that
is granted you under the sun. (9:7,9)

The final verses of his book rescue Qoheleth from
the groundless charges of pessimism and hedonism:

The last word, when all is heard:
Fear God and keep his commandments,
for this is man's all. (12:13)

One of the commandments of God is that his
creatures should work: "Fill the earth and subdue it"
(Genesis 1:28); "The Lord God then took the man and
settled him in the garden of Eden, to cultivate and care
for it" (Genesis 2:15). If our purpose in life is to care for
the earth, work is surely our normal activity on earth.
What a contrast with the Greek concept of work, which
saw work as fitting only for slaves! In Judaism it was a
charge entrusted by God.

God himself works. The Jewish Scriptures tell how
God spread out the heavens like a tent (Isaiah 40:22),
how he created man like a potter moulding clay
(Genesis 2:7) and woman like a sculptor building on a
rib (Genesis 2:22). God also planted a garden (Genesis
2:8); made leather garments for the man and his wife
(Genesis 3:21); wrote (Exodus 31:18); closed the door of
the ark (Genesis 7:16); and even buried Moses
(Deuteronomy 34:6).

Our task is to share in God's creative work by
continuing it. To the extent that we do, God gives good
outcome and successful accomplishment to our labor:

Unless the Lord build the house,
they labor in vain who build it. . . .
It is vain for you to rise early,
or put off your rest,
You that eat hard-earned bread,
for he gives to his beloved in sleep.
(Psalm 127:1-2)

This is why the pious Jew prays for God's blessing on his work and thanks him for its successful completion. In antiquity, the Jew offered firstfruits and tithes of crops and livestock to God as a sign of thanksgiving (Deuteronomy 14:22-29).

Work became hard, painful, and puzzling when the first parents disobeyed God, but God promised to redeem them from its hardship. God's special redemption occurred in the Exodus. In Egypt the Jew was a slave, condemned to work at a pitiless pace, under harsh supervision with cruel beatings, among a hostile people, for the profit of an enemy government. Such treatment was actually part of a systematic effort to weaken resistance and to annihilate a people.

But God led his people out of this situation into a land flowing with milk and honey where he blessed their labor and allowed them to eat the fruit of their own work, so long as they were faithful to the Covenant (Deuteronomy 30:15-20). The Sabbath and feastday observances gave them a respite from work and allowed them to rest as God rested (Genesis 2:3; Exodus 20:8-11). In Judaism, work is not the be-all and end-all of life for God's creatures.

The Jewish test for wellness, therefore, is fidelity to God's will, for it is God who has put purpose and meaning into life. Qoheleth and others like him may strive to fathom this purpose and meaning, and that is praiseworthy. But it remains elusive, and in the long run keeping God's commandments and continuing his creative care for this world constitute life's greatest pleasures and single purpose—and lead to the highest levels of wellness.[7]

A CHRISTIAN TEST FOR WELLNESS

One day Jesus said: "I came that they might have life and have it to the full." Full life has been the goal of his followers throughout the ages. In the context of John's Gospel, where this passage is recorded (10:10), full life means nothing less than a share in the life of God himself.

You can share this full life by being born from above (John 3), by becoming a branch on the Vine which is Jesus (John 15), because he is the "way and the truth and the life" (John 14:6) or, as a modern biblical scholar translates it, "the authentic vision of existence."

All the gospels, indeed all the Christian Scriptures, strive to explain what the fullness of life promised by Jesus means and how to achieve it. Because he and his original followers were Jews, they—like Qoheleth— sought their self-understanding in the Jewish Scriptures. This was the source that could help them express their own growing self-understanding and their new insights into the purpose and meaning of life.

One day Jesus returned to Nazareth, where he had grown up, and entered the synagogue to join in the service (Luke 4:16-17).[8] He was invited to read the Scriptures. Unrolling the scroll of the prophet Isaiah, he found this passage and read it:

> *The spirit of the Lord GOD is upon me,*
> *   because the LORD has anointed me;*
> *He has sent me to bring glad tidings to the lowly,*
> *   to heal the brokenhearted,*
> *To proclaim liberty to the captives*
> *   and release to the prisoners,*
> *To announce a year of favor from the LORD*
> *   and a day of vindication by our GOD,*
> *To comfort all who mourn. (Isaiah 61:1-2)*

When he sat down again he began his commentary by noting "Today this Scripture passage is fulfilled in your hearing" (Luke 4:21). At first his comments amazed his listeners, but then they became angry and expelled him from his own home town.

After the death of Jesus, his disciples discussed his teachings and preachings and reflected on the Jewish Scriptures which they continued to hear in the synagogues. They seem to have cherished this passage from Isaiah, because it appears more than once in the Christian Scriptures. They even adapted it as they referred to it. For instance, the Isaiah passage quoted above is from the Hebrew text. Luke's actual report is slightly different:

> *The spirit of the Lord is upon me;*
> *Therefore he has anointed me.*
> *He has sent me to bring glad tidings*
> *to the poor,*
> *to proclaim liberty to the captives,*
> *Recovery of sight to the blind*
> *and release to prisoners. (Luke 4:18-19)*

Luke moulded the passage to express his understanding.

Another reference to the passage echoes in the reply given by Jesus to the disciples of John sent to ask whether Jesus was the one who was to come, or whether they should look for another.

> "Go and report to John what you have seen and heard. The blind recover their sight, cripples walk, lepers are cured, the deaf hear, dead men are raised to life, and the poor have the good news preached to them." He added: "Blest is that man who finds no stumbling block in me." (Luke 7:22-23)

The most striking interpretation of these verses in Isaiah appears in the Beatitudes of Matthew and Luke. There is no doubt that they were inspired by and modeled after the Isaiah passage.

Beatitudes are very common in Scripture. A beatitude is a poetic saying used to express a culturally valuable attitude or line of conduct. Because it is a poetic saying, it must be treated as poetry and appreciated as poetry. People who don't relate well to poetry will likely find difficulty relating to beatitudes.

Beatitudes first appear in the Jewish Scriptures that were written after the exile, that is, after the year 587 before the Common Era. Two kinds of beatitudes have been identified: wisdom, and apocalyptic. A wisdom beatitude praises something here and now valuable for *present* well-being.

For instance, Psalm 127: 4-5 observes:

> *Like arrows in the hand of a warrior*
> *are the sons of one's youth;*
> *Happy the man whose quiver is filled*
> *with them;*
> *they shall not be put to shame*
> *when they contend*
> *with enemies at the gate.*

Such obvious advice is hardly startling: Raise children because they can come in handy. Sons in this culture were particularly valuable since they could help you in court (the gate is where legal activity took place, as in our court).

The apocalyptic beatitude praised a here-and-now attitude or line of conduct that is valuable for *future* well-being. Because the connection of the present action to future well-being was not always obvious, this type of beatitude frequently needed a motive clause ("for . . . ," "because . . . "). Tobit's song of praise promised:

> *Happy are those who love you [Jerusalem],*
> *and happy those who rejoice in your prosperity.*
> *Happy are all men who shall grieve over you,*
> *over all your chastisements,*
> *For they shall rejoice in you*
> *as they behold all your joy forever.* (Tobit 13:14)

This same kind of beatitude or blessing is found in the gospels and other Christian Scriptures. "Happy that servant," says Jesus in his parable, "whom his master discovers at work on his return! I assure you, he will put him in charge of all his property" (Matthew 24:46-47). The book of Revelation notes: "Happy now are the dead who die in the Lord! . . . . Yes, they shall find rest from their labors, for their good works accompany them" (Revelation 14:13).

The gospel beatitudes in fact go beyond these simple statements and announce a complete reversal of circumstances. This is particularly true of the most familiar beatitudes, those of Matthew's Sermon on the Mount and Luke's Sermon on the Plain.

Luke's first three beatitudes are very likely the original beatitudes spoken by Jesus. These three sum up the meaning and purpose of life as Jesus taught it, as his followers preached it, and as the Evangelists recorded it.

> *Blest are you poor, the reign of God is yours.*
> *Blest are you who hunger, you shall be filled.*
> *Blest are you who are weeping, you shall laugh.*
> *(Luke 6:20-21)*

The complete reversal of circumstances promised by Jesus is unmistakable in these three beatitudes. Luke, who is concerned about the poor and oppressed as a social class, gives them encouragement and hope. The "theological passives" in these sayings assure such people that *God* will change their fortune. (God, whose name could not be pronounced, is always understood to be the agent of the verb in the passive voice in the Bible when the question "By whom?" doesn't have any other answer in the text or context.)

It is Matthew who expands the Beatitudes to eight and who also broadens the horizons. He moves beyond the actual state of a person to consider the attitudes,

outlooks, behaviors, and values appropriate to a follower
of Jesus. Any attempt to do his work justice has to be a
poetic attempt. The following paraphrase is one such
attempt.

> *Blessed are you, poor . . . in spirit (Jesus said).*
> *You who cringe from oppression,*
> *who are doubled up to protect yourself*
> *from further blows,*
> *who are weak, powerless, and defenseless*
> *in the system.*
> *Indeed, blessed are you in such a state,*
> *BUT ONLY IF together with this condition,*
> *you are also open to God,*
> *you remain loyal to him,*
> *convinced that he alone*
> *can satisfy your yearnings,*
> *can fill your needs,*
> *can lead you to the full life.*
> *Yes, even if you are not actually poor,*
> *but you realize it is only God that*
> *makes sense out of life,*
> *You—rich or poor—are pleasing to God,*
> *and God himself will see to your cause.*
> *AND AGAIN,*
> *Blessed are you who hunger and thirst,*
> *thirst for righteousness,*
> *who long for a life approved by God,*
> *a life definitively,*
> *once-and-for-always*
> *set free from all oppression;*
> *who yearn fervently for God to establish*
> *his reign over all the world,*
> *his will over all people,*
> *who make this the focus of your social*
> *concern, of your prayer.*
> *I, Jesus, myself give you my word as pledge;*

you will not be disappointed.
AND YET AGAIN,
Blessed are you who weep and sorrow,
who mourn,
that is, you who adopt the protest pattern
because this world is closed to God . . .
because the community of Christian
believers
is defiled,
falls short of the holiness
that God demands.
Indeed, blessed are you who take firm action
to remove the arrogant sinner from your
midst,
to tear out the evil from among you.
Yes, God will wipe your tears,
restore your cheer,
and bless your efforts with success.

This is not a passive program of life. There is a clear emphasis on action, on a committed and vigorous response to the challenge posed by this view of life's purpose and meaning. For most Christians it requires a change of heart, a "conversion," an outlook different from the one generally suggested by society and culture. But the payoff is vastly more satisfying and fulfilling than you can even begin to imagine.

Jesus spent almost all of his own life in manual labor. He was a carpenter (Mark 6:3), considered to be the son of a carpenter. He introduced no new ideas on work in his teachings but clearly approved the value placed upon it in the Jewish Scriptures. His life shows that. At the same time, he cautioned against making work the sole purpose in life. He pointed to the lilies of the field that didn't spin or toil but were more beautiful than the finest products money could buy. He told the story of the man who thought he'd save the fruits of his labor and get rich but who died prematurely, never to

enjoy his retirement plan. Jesus said to seek God's will
and purpose and everything else would fall into place.

It was Paul who gave a new Christian interpretation
to work. He described it as a service rendered not so
much to men as to God.

> Do not render service for appearance only and to
> please men, but do God's will with your whole
> heart as slaves of Christ. Give your service
> willingly, doing it for the Lord rather than men.
> You know that each one, whether slave or free, will
> be repaid by the Lord for whatever good he does.
> (Ephesians 6:6-8)

The Christian test for wellness suggested by Jesus
and his followers does not ask Christians to be the
world's doormats (despite what Szasz claims). It does not
encourage laziness nor excuse a person from serious
concern about the society and culture in which he or
she lives. The Christian test for wellness forces a
believer to determine whether his or her life's purpose
and goal square with that proposed by God for creation.
The norm and measure is the example of Jesus, the
quality and direction of the life of Jesus, particularly as
captured in the Beatitudes.

Francis, the Poor Man of Assisi, understood this
perfectly, lived it faithfully, and made it part of the rule
for his followers: "When the friars are blessed by the
Lord with ability in some form of work, they should do
their work faithfully and out of a sense of dedication"
(Rule, Chapter 5).

Echoing the biblical tradition, Francis sees work as
a gift from God, as human participation in God's
creative work. "Sense of dedication" is his way of saying
that his followers should recognize the value of work as
an external demonstration of the internal understanding
and acceptance of God's designs and will for creation.

It was this viewpoint that made Francis very impatient with the friar who never showed up for work but always showed up to eat. He said:

> "Go your way, Brother Fly: For you wish only to consume what your brethren have obtained by their honest sweat and to be niggardly in the work of God. You are like Brother Drone, who shares not the labor of the bees, yet is the first to eat the honey."[9]

At the same time as he urged his followers to work, Francis also cautioned them that the important thing was to be on guard "not thereby to destroy the spirit of holy prayer and devotedness. For to this inner spirit all other things of life must positively contribute" (*Rule*, Chapter 5). It was this that transformed work from a purely profit-making venture into a genuine contribution to building the kingdom of God and to establishing his reign in the world.

Francis' observation on the role of work in life and its relationship to prayer is a key measure of wellness for the Christian. In his day, when the city-states were flourishing in Italy and placing increased emphasis on commerce and wealth, everybody wanted to work. The problem was that work became an obsession for many and locked all other activity and purpose out of life. Unlike the monks who worked in their monasteries, Francis and his followers went out and worked among the people. Francis realized that the people did not need to learn how to work, but rather how to pray and meditate, and how to see work as the human contribution to the divine plans.

In too many persons, including Christians, work and prayer, work and the totality of the Christ-life are separated and departmentalized. On Sunday, the Bible is their ledger; on weekdays, the ledger is their Bible.

Francis urged not only that prayer, spirituality, and all of life be appropriately coordinated, but also that they be integrated into a whole. Wellness educators who call for the daily practice of centering and a regular period of meditation are simply re-discovering an element that has strong roots in the Christian tradition.

CONCLUSION[10]

Article XI of the 1936 Constitution of the Union of Soviet Socialist Republics quotes the proverb "Anyone who would not work should not eat." It is unlikely that the Soviets borrowed it from Paul's second letter to the Thessalonians 3:10, where it is also quoted. The wide diffusion of this proverb simply points out the number and variety of people who have believed that work is life's sole purpose and meaning.

Testing for wellness means nothing less than asking whether one's outlook on life is fitting and whether there isn't more to life than the outlook expresses.

The humanistic wellness educator has no problem with work so long as it contributes to human growth and development, for that is the supreme value of life in a humanist perspective. Work is defined as modifying the human environment for the purpose of human growth and development.

The Jewish test for wellness of life's meaning and purpose explores the degree to which a person realizes a unique and individual share in God's creative work. Work is simply a part of this; so too is leisure. Jewish wellness knows how to balance the two.

The Christian also accepts this viewpoint and recognizes Jesus' challenge to culture and its assumptions. The Christian notes that work is an especially fitting part of life's meaning and purpose if it serves others, builds God's kingdom and stirs acceptance of his reign, and contributes to the true welfare of creation.

The Franciscan expression of Christian spirituality adds that work fits admirably into life's meaning and purpose provided that it doesn't extinguish the spirit of prayer and devotion.

Christians and Jews alike believe that God has set the meaning of life and that his will is its purpose. The next question is: Can this view be fun? Can it make for a pleasurable and enjoyable life? It is to this aspect of wellness that we now turn our attention.

NOTES

1. See The General Mills American Family Report, 1976-1977, *Raising Children in a Changing Society* (Minneapolis, Minn: General Mills, Inc., 1977) for details. An application of wellness insights to this data as well as reflections on the relationship of Christian outlooks to this data can be heard on two audio-cassettes: *The Energized Family* and *Family Wellness* (Kansas City, Mo.: NCR Cassettes).

2. For information about the Wellness Inventory write to Dr. Travis at 42 Miller Avenue, Mill Valley, CA 94941.

3. Available from Psychometric Affiliates, P.O. Box 3167, Munster, IN 46321. If you like "tests" of this kind, you may like the book *Understanding Yourself*, with an introduction by Dr. Christopher Evans (New York: A & W Publishers, 1977), especially "Are You a Happy Human?" and "Are You in the Right Job?"

4. Of the many value-clarification materials available, a clear and simple-to-use booklet is *Deciding for Myself: A Values-Clarification Series*, developed by Wayne Paulson (Minneapolis, Minn: Winston Press, 1974).

5. For an excellent understanding of Americans, study Robin M. Williams, Jr., *American Society: A Sociological Interpretation*, 3rd edition (New York: Alfred A. Knopf, 1970), acknowledged to be the best resource on this subject. Of particular interest to this chapter are Williams' Chapter XI, "Values in American Society," pp. 438-504, and Chapter VI, "American Economic Institutions," pp. 166-230.

6. I base this outline on the masterful study by Addison G. Wright, "The Riddle of the Sphinx: The Structure of the Book of Qoheleth," *Catholic Biblical Quarterly* 30 (1968): 313-34. It is the outline adopted by the *New American Bible* translators and very recently strengthened by Wright's continued research as reported in "The Riddle of the Sphinx Revisited: Numerical Patterns in the Book of Qoheleth," *Catholic Biblical Quarterly* 42 (1980): 38-51. The development of my ideas may also betray the influence of Rabbi Robert Gordis, *Koheleth—The Man and His World*, rev. ed. (New York: Schocken, 1967), whom I read with keen interest and respect when I was a graduate student.

7. For another perspective on the place of work in human life and its meaning and purpose in human existence, see "Works" in the *Foundations Cassette Series* (Kansas City, Mo.: NCR Cassettes) which uses John's Gospel as a focal point.

8. In this section, I develop my presentation in line with the principles used by all Catholic scholars as recorded in the 1964 Instruction of the Pontifical Biblical Commission "Concerning the Historical Truth of the Gospels." That document was cited again briefly by the Second Vatican Council's *Dogmatic Constitution on Revelation*, n. 19. The principles are substantially identical with those used by other Christian biblical scholars for decades prior to these two documents.

9. 2 Celano, n. 75. Thomas Celano's second biography of Francis (usually referred to as 2 Celano) can be found in numerous editions. Those who are interested in a major source book should consult *St. Francis of Assisi: Writings and Early Biographies: English Omnibus of the Sources for the Life of St. Francis*, ed. Marion A. Habig (Chicago: Franciscan Herald Press, 1972).

10. A wellness perspective on work as part of a larger Christian wellness spirituality can be heard in the audio-cassette "Making Life and Work One," in the program *Ministry and Wellness: A Holistic Approach* (Kansas City, Mo.: NCR Cassettes, 1979). Yet another development of the themes of this chapter can be heard in the audio-cassette program "Parish Wellness: Renewal for the 1980's" in the presentation entitled *The Meaning of Life* (Kansas City, Mo.: NCR Cassettes, 1980).

CHAPTER FOUR

WELLNESS AND LIFE'S PLEASURES

Auntie Mame declared, "Life is a banquet, but most poor suckers are starving to death!" The wellness movement is inviting people back to the banquet, encouraging them to take their hearty share of life, to pursue life to the full.

Earlier I identified the leading causes of sickness and premature death among Americans as stemming from Life-Style Five:

- excessive eating of both appropriate and unhealthy foods;
- excessive drinking of health-destructive beverages;
- excessive smoking;
- insufficient physical exercise;
- unmanaged stress.

Professional health educators have long known and repeatedly suggested counter-elements for a healthier lifestyle:

- more reflective nutritional awareness;

- adequate physical fitness;
- more effective control of stress and its causes;
- enhanced environmental sensitivity;
- increased self-responsibility.

Specific details of each of these life-style elements are commonly known and readily available from a variety of sources. Much begins with plain common sense. At least some proper eating habits are begun in the family circle. Additional information is taught in the school system. The food section of the daily newspaper regularly carries basic information about shopping for, preparing, and eating a balanced and healthy diet. But Americans seem to know more about what their cars need than about what their own bodies need.

We also know the damage to our health by our drinking habits. The old water-cooler in nearly all office workplaces has been replaced by the ever-perking coffeepot. Employees gather here during the day to share personal items about family, health, neighborhood, films, and take coffee back to their desks to sip throughout the day. It is not uncommon for people to refill their cup at 4:30 and 4:45 of a day that ends at 5:00. Visitors too are offered coffee whether their appointment is at an early or a late hour. And yet excessive coffee drinking can be as damaging as excessive alcoholic consumption.

There is no need to review the damage of our alcoholic-drinking habits. It is, however, very sobering to realize that nearly ten percent of the work force is seriously enough addicted to be identified as alcoholics. These workers not only damage their own health but reduce industrial output and become a liability by excessive absences and a decreasing level of efficiency. The effect of excessive drinking outside the work force is just as serious, particularly for home life.

Our failure to maintain physical fitness is somewhat ironic, considering that sport activity in this country is almost a civil religion. Emphasis on fitness programs for youth dwindles as people grow older and become more involved in the work world, homemaking, or other areas of human activity that either do not require much exertion or offer little time for a fitness program.

Common and popular means for dealing with stress include excessive smoking, alcohol, and other drugs. It is rarely noted that these elements deal mainly with the symptoms of stress and not with the problems causing it. Perhaps this is why Americans commonly prefer chemical management of stress. Increased interest in meditation and relaxation techniques, however, signals a welcome change from the common pattern.

Environmental sensitivity relates to stress, too, though most people think of environment in terms of ecology: clear water, fresh air, pollution control. But environment also includes human components: fellow human beings and the effect they have on us and we on them. A noontime martini may be a source of courage to return to a job you hate, supervised by a boss who irritates you. In addition you brood as you wonder how your fellow-worker always seems able to whistle while she works while you see nothing to whistle about. A healthier life-style demands facing environmental problems squarely and doing something about them.

All the alternative elements for healthier life-style hinge on self-responsibility, self-care. Probably nothing you've read so far in this chapter is new to you; both print and electronic media have called these truths to your attention. Perhaps even friends, relatives, or counselors (physicians, clergy, and the like) have suggested a change in your life-style.

But knowledge is not virtue; knowing the proper course of action doesn't guarantee that you will adopt it. Professional health educators will not hesitate to admit that they have been very minimally effective in their programs. Children in school can rattle off all the appropriate habits for good living, but they still skip breakfast, prefer junk food for lunch, and make sure they get their smoke breaks between classes. No universally effective source of motivating everyone to opt for the full life, to seek a place at the banquet of life, has yet been found.

I believe, however, that wellness education can succeed where traditional health education has faltered: It can motivate you to assume more responsibility for your own life and well-being. I believe that spiritual values and religious beliefs provide some of the strongest motives for revising a health-destructive life-style or strengthening a life-affirming one if you so desire, because they relate to two facts that health educators know but fail to address effectively: the importance of self-esteem, and the importance of values.

It is widely known and accepted that the people most likely to initiate and maintain a health-promoting life-style are those who have a high sense of self-esteem. Anyone interested in motivating others to change their individual life-styles will be much more successful by addressing self-esteem rather than by merely relating accurate information.

A second very important insight came from a survey of the members of the American Public Health Association. The survey revealed that health professionals tended to base their life-styles not on what they knew, but on their values.[1] Health educators increasingly realize that any knowledge they want to transmit must be related to the values of their audience in order to be effective.

Thus wellness education that roots itself in spiritual values or values drawn from religious traditions can be very effective in pointing out, in this chapter for example, that life is a banquet (in a figurative as well as a literal sense). Wellness does invite you to come to the banquet of life, to take your full and hearty share.

In the following pages I will show how spiritual values and religious beliefs can strengthen your resolution to adopt a healthier life-style in pursuit of a full, purposeful, and pleasurable life, a life of high-level wellness. I will use the element of more reflective nutritional awareness as the focus for the chapter.

THE BANQUET OF LIFE: A HUMANISTIC PERSPECTIVE

Americans have not been totally unaware of the fact that life is a banquet. Taking the narrow focus on food alone, the U.S. problem is essentially one of overconsumption and undernutrition. At least five of the ten leading causes of death in America are diet-related: heart disease; cardio-vascular diseases; diabetes mellitus; arteriosclerosis; cirrhosis of the liver. We would do well to recall the Irish proverb:

Leave the table hungry,
leave the tavern thirsty,
leave the bed sleepy.

But by itself the proverb rings too simply of asceticism and self-denial—and negative approaches are rarely if ever successful.

Wellness takes a positive approach; it focuses on the meaning and pleasure of eating. It urges that the very act of eating be linked to your sense of life's purpose, meaning, and pleasure. Folk wisdom advises: "Eat to live; don't live to eat!" And those who would call your attention to bad eating habits frequently observe that you're "eating like there's no tomorrow" or "like it's going out of style." In the Polish neighborhoods of my youth, we children were often quoted the phrase: "A bogiem ich był brzuch," whose translation "and their belly was their god" suggested that we were filling our stomachs with food as if we were offering sacrifices to a god.

One way to take a positive approach to life and to pursue wellness in the best humanistic tradition is to take a creative outlook on life's purpose, meaning, and pleasure. Creativity can be defined in many ways, but it is perhaps most keenly captured in the familiar observation "Some people see things as they are and ask why. Others think things that are not and ask why not." Asking "Why not?" gives creativity at least two roles in wellness: pragmatism, and fulfillment.

From a pragmatic perspective, life can be enjoyable if its ordinary activities can be carried out effectively and with little or no impediment. For example, consider how much easier cooking can be if you have all the pots, pans, utensils and other equipment you need. Imagine, too, how much more enjoyable it can be if the kitchen is arranged for efficient operation, with a work center boasting coordination among the stove, sink, and refrigerator—the three main points of meal preparation.

And while kneading bread is good exercise, particularly for hypertensives, other persons such as arthritics are grateful for the time-saving and effort-reducing power tools like electric mixers, blenders, and food processors. From this viewpoint you can understand why Marriage Encounter exercises ask you to identify whether the kitchen (or any other place) is an area of pleasure or conflict. The answer reveals a lot about your wellness—your pleasurable, purposeful life.

In our time the kitchen has once more become the center of activity in the home. This has considerably reduced the kitchen's potential for conflict. Not many years ago, before central heating was common, nearly everything took place in the kitchen: Children did homework at the kitchen table (there was room for only a bed and dresser in the bedroom); meals, of course, were eaten at this same table; the insurance man collected the premium at this table; and the family sat around the table after dishes to read, discuss, or listen to the radio. The modern move back to the kitchen has prompted some observers to suggest we rename it the living room, because that is what it has become. No one need ever feel condemned to the kitchen, or isolated in it. This new or restored function of the room puts a new and satisfying perspective on the various tasks and activities that take place there.

Another wellness dimension of modern living is the trend to combine eating and leisure. It is not uncommon to take meals around the TV (not TV dinners!) when mealtime coincides with a special that's of interest to the entire family. We also hold barbecues at poolside or on the patio, where we share fellowship as well as nourishment. There is even a somewhat new activity known as the tailgate party: a picnic in the stadium parking lot, not in the stands.

As food preparation and eating have merged with leisure, sociability, and broad personal fulfillment activities in the home, they have regained popularity and significance as family activities. They have, in fact, become key elements of family wellness. Statistics indicate that four in ten mothers and two in ten fathers believe that eating together—in peaceful and loving harmony—has a positive effect on the nutritional benefits to be gained from good food, no matter what the menu.

But there is another way of exercising creativity in developing a pleasurable and enjoyable life, and I call that fulfilling creativity. In the specific area of cooking and eating, no one—in my judgment—has demonstrated this kind of creativity better than Robert Farrar Capon, Episcopalian priest-author of *The Supper of the Lamb*.[2] There is no doubt that Capon's introduction to the joys of real cooking are at the same time a subtle introduction to the joys of real living.

His book is actually a recipe for lamb served four times for eight persons. As he unfolds the recipe in each

chapter, he shares his reflections, going beyond the
ingredients and the process to the planning and
arrangment of the dinner party at which the completed
dish will be served.

Capon's eye for pleasure is revealed in his
comments on how many guests to invite to the dinner.
(So what if the recipe is for eight?) First, you ought to
have at least one solidly personal reason for inviting
whomever you summon to your table—and it should
not be a business reason. For this there are the
restaurant and the cocktail hour. Your home table is
where you want to share love.

Secondly, try to invite people who will enhance one
another as persons. And when you have selected them,
begin immediately to imagine them seated in carefully
selected places at your table. As you further recall their
reciprocities, you may mentally move the guests about,
but settle on the seating plan as soon as is convenient.

You cannot make dinner company of just any
number of people. Accordingly, in your planning,
put down eight as the optimum number and vary
from it only for good reasons. Four persons, if they
are all unmarried, is a possibility; but two couples is
not, save under unusual circumstances such as first
friendship or reunion after long separation. Six is
better, especially with couples who see each other
occasionally, since it provides not only variety, but
also a physical arrangement by which no one,
except the host, sits either next to, or across from
his own wife. Eight, as I said, is ideal. It is large
enough to allow for considerable interplay between
personalities, yet it is still small enough to permit
the serving of some of the most elegant dishes of
all. . . . Larger groupings are sometimes desirable,
but they become difficult for various reasons. Ten is
gala, but it rules out not only the souffle, but

almost anything from the broiler. Twelve is sumptuous, but it tends to breed isolated conversations at opposite ends of the table and so imperils the very company it sets out to form. After that, however, any greater number has so many drawbacks that it precludes a true dinner altogether. (p. 173)

Yet Capon is not insensitive to the fact that there may indeed be festal occasions that call for larger numbers of people. He continues:

For such a crowd, it would be better to plan a completely different party: a splendid buffet, for example, with guests imaginatively assigned to tables of four each, and with provision for dancing and general clowning afterward. As with all things, it is a matter of paying attention to what you have in hand. (p. 173)

Capon's last sentence sums up the humanistic approach to enhancing the enjoyable dimensions of a wellness life-style. What is at hand is human life and unique persons. Creativity is one way of enhancing the uniqueness of life and persons and heightening the pleasure and enjoyment that should be had from whatever is at hand: food, eating, people, or any human activity.

THE BANQUET OF LIFE: A JEWISH PERSPECTIVE

The preceding pages of this book should have made it abundantly clear that the Jew sees life as having purpose and meaning and as giving great pleasure. These characteristics are intertwined and can be illustrated by the Jewish outlooks on food and eating. We will

consider two examples: the kosher laws, and the
Sabbath meals.

My first conscious encounter with the kosher laws
came as a youngster. (Unreflective encounters must
certainly have taken place sooner, since my parents were
superintendents of a large apartment building in Boro
Park, a Jewish neighborhood in Brooklyn, where my
playmates frequently invited me to supper.)

One day when my brothers and I accompanied my
dad on a shopping trip to the lower East Side of New
York, we went to Katz's Delicatessen for lunch. The
waiter at the counter beamed at my dad and at us three
boys. Each of us got a kosher pickle even before we
ordered. As the Good Book says,

> *Behold, sons are a gift from the Lord. . . .*
> *Like arrows in the hand of a warrior are the*
>   *sons of one's youth. (Psalm 127:3-4)*

When the waiter asked for our order, my dad said:
"Four kosher corned beef sandwiches on rye bread with
mustard and another pickle." Then the waiter asked
what we'd like to drink, and he looked down at us boys
for an answer. "A glass of milk, please," I said. My dad
corrected me: "He'll have a bottle of celery soda, with a
glass, please." The waiter smiled as I looked at my dad
in anguish. I'd never heard of celery soda before. Why
couldn't I have milk? I did say "Please." He must have
understood, but he motioned me to keep silent.

Later, at the table, Dad explained one of the Jewish
kosher laws to me: Never mix the *milchiks* with the
fleischiks at one meal (Yiddish words signifying dairy
products and meat). He didn't exactly know why, but
he knew it was a law, and here in the kosher restaurant
he felt we should observe it, too. I received a basic
lesson not only in Judaism but in ecumenism long
before the word and practice came into fashion.

Many years afterward I learned that this law is based on the interpretation of Exodus 23:19: "You shall not boil a kid in its mother's milk." To many a modern non-believer this is primitive superstition, unscientific, and irrational. To a Jew this and all the kosher laws highlight not only the meaning of eating but the very meaning and purpose of life itself.

Rabbis offer at least three reasons why these kosher laws are still worth observing. First, they are an exercise in maintaining holiness before God. The list of clean and unclean (kosher and treif) foods in Leviticus 11:1-43 concludes with this comment: "For I, the LORD, am your God; and you shall make and keep yourselves holy, because I am holy" (11:44). This is why the believer must distinguish between clean and unclean, and between creatures that may be eaten and those that may not. The holiness commandment is repeated throughout the Torah. Therefore obeying these kosher laws is a commandment, a miṣwah. They are intended for ritual purity but also for maintaining a proper relationship between God and yourself.

A second reason for keeping the kosher laws is to learn self-control. Sometimes the freedom gained in the Exodus can be like heady wine: It can lead to license. The rabbis teach that the kosher laws provide some discipline in a life of freedom. By observing the laws appropriately we can become masters of our lives, our selves, our bodies, our desires. We increase our self-responsibility and self-determination. We are not controlled by creatures, but faithful to our charge at creation, we become masters of all that exists (Genesis 1:26,28). This outlook meshes admirably with the basic definition of wellness.

A third reason for keeping the kosher laws is to show reverence and respect for life. It is a willingness to accept responsibility for life before God and humanity. The Jewish tradition believes that in the beginning God created us to be vegetarians. God said:

"See, I give you every seed-bearing plant all over
the earth and every tree that has seed-bearing fruit
on it to be your food; and to all the animals of the
land, all the birds of the air, and all the living
creatures that crawl on the ground, I give all the
green plants for food." (Genesis 1:29-30)

It wasn't until after the Flood that God allowed
Noah and his survivors to eat meat. But he phrased the
permission very carefully:

"Every creature that is alive shall be yours to eat; I
give them all to you as I did the green plants. Only
flesh with its lifeblood still in it you shall not eat.
For your own lifeblood, too, I will demand an
accounting: from every animal I will demand it,
and from man in regard to his fellow man I will
demand an accounting for human life."
(Genesis 9:3-5)

This passage is the basis for the special process of
slaughtering an animal (sheḥiṭah) as well as kashering
(soaking and salting) the meat. Both processes emphasize
the sanctity of life, all life. No one may eat an animal
that has been torn apart (ṭerepah) or one that has died a
natural death (nebalah) (Leviticus 7:24). (The Yiddish
word for unkosher food is treif, derived from the
Hebrew word just mentioned: ṭerepah, meaning "torn
apart.") Thus the human pleasure of eating must always
be related to the sacred dimension of all life.
   Yet the Jewish understanding of these laws is not
inflexible. The tradition has no place of eternal
punishment for those who do not observe the laws. And
the rabbis discuss an interesting case of a pregnant
woman who suddenly gets a terrible and abiding craving
for roast pork. What to do? Well, let her smell the
aroma of pork roasting. If that doesn't satisfy the

yearning, let her dip her finger into the drippings and
taste. If that still doesn't satisfy the yearning, let her
touch the meat and taste her finger. If nothing satisfies,
let her finally eat the roast pork, since the greatest
obligation for a Jew is to save life.

A second example of the pleasure a Jew finds in life
is the observance of the Sabbath, a word deriving from
the Hebrew verb *shabat*, meaning "to cease working, to
rest." The Bible relates the word to the seventh day,
when God rested from his work of creation. God's
creatures are urged to do the same. Thus Sabbath rest is
a very important feature of Jewish life, for it is a weekly
reminder and opportunity to enjoy life, to reflect on the
real pleasures of living. It is definitely a key element of a
high-level wellness life-style for Jews.

Even Moses noted that untempered observance of
the Genesis command to subdue the earth and have
dominion over it could be disastrous (Deuteronomy 8).
You could begin to take excessive pride in your own
accomplishments, completely forget about God, and
become a workaholic. The Sabbath helps you keep
everything in proper perspective.

Though the Sabbath officially is only one day, from
Friday twilight to Saturday evening, its observance
actually covers the entire week. Preparations begin on
Wednesday, and the Sabbath ending extends even as far
as Tuesday.

Preparation is very important to enjoying anything
in life. Sabbath is no different. Some people take a
special purificatory bath (a *miqweh*) to begin the holiday
with a clean soul, a new life. Others set aside time to
read the Torah portion for the week. (Torah is read in
the synagogue on Monday and Thursday as well as on
the Sabbath.) And still others take time for meditation,
for reviewing the week gone by to gradually free the
mind of its cares, worries, and concerns.

The holiday itself is a time for refreshment, for

resouling the world—a theme relating to creation. Proper observance of the day will make you feel as if you have a new soul, and when the day ends, you will feel that special soul leave. Sabbath is a very special occasion for taking time to do what was ignored or perhaps rushed during the week. It is a special time for sharing love, above all conjugal love. Friday evening is particularly a sensual time: a time for good eating, pleasant candlelight, family singing, subdued talk, and enjoyment of the physical as well as spiritual love of the family.

Saturday is a time for Torah study and reflection on the commandments, the will of God. These two elements are reflected in the popular names for the Sabbath: Bride (*Kallah*) and Queen (*Malkah*). In the days of preparation, the family observes "The Queen is coming" and asks "How shall we greet the Bride?" As Bride, the Sabbath symbolizes love, devotion, and feeling. As Queen, the Sabbath reminds you to obey the Torah, to study it, to learn it and keep its commandments.

The final ceremony on Saturday evening, the *Havdalah*, separates this holy time from the coming week, though it invites you to carry over the Sabbath sentiment into that week. Describing these observances comes nowhere near capturing their total beauty and significance. If you are not Jewish, get yourself invited to a Sabbath meal. Don't worry, you won't be imposing; it's a *miṣwah* (a commandment) to host guests on the Sabbath. You'll gain a valuable insight into some basic Jewish elements of a high-level wellness life style, particularly the efforts Jews make to review, appreciate, and intensify the true pleasures of life.

THE BANQUET OF LIFE: A CHRISTIAN PERSPECTIVE

On the night before he died, Jesus sat down to supper with the Apostles, his intimate friends. The Christian

Scriptures identify the meal as a Passover celebration, which in Judaism has always been a happy celebration of liberation from slavery in Egypt. That meal is one of the happiest that Jews eat.

The gospel context certainly echoes the significance of the Passover meal in the life of Jesus, but it appears to have muted the joyful dimensions. The Christian eucharistic traditions that developed from this Last Supper not only continued to restrain the joyful dimension but in many cases even lost any resemblance to a meal.

In Christianity, the pleasure and joy of the banquet which is life is the unexpected discovery you make in life's reversals, in what is called the paschal mystery: the mystery of growing to new life out of daily deaths.[3] It is not surprising, then, to note that instead of waiting for these reversals, Christians began to anticipate them in varied ways. With special reference to the topic of food and eating, Christians developed a tradition of fasting.

Contemporary wellness educators are delighted to learn this, because they enthusiastically promote fasting as a significant element in a wellness life-style. In a humanistic perspective on wellness, fasting serves to purify the body and restore an appreciation of foods to the one who fasts. One wellness educator said he was very interested in introducing fasting into his life-style but would want an experienced guide to observe and monitor his activities lest he do harm to his health.

Certainly many Catholics would be more than willing to serve as his experienced guides. Recent Catholic fasting has been restrained and not at all like the Ramadan (no food till nightfall). The basic Catholic rule since 1918 is that you may eat one full meal on a fast day. The other two meals should not equal the amount of food in your full meal. Nibbling between meals to ease hunger pains is allowed if the amount does

not add up to four ounces. This latter rule should not
be pressed too literally, since fasting is relative to the
constitution of the individual person.

In the course of my education, we were encouraged
to become acquainted with the quantity of four ounces
of salt (mainly its weight) so as to have some reference
point for four ounces. You'd be surprised how much
popcorn, pretzels, or potato chips it takes to make up
four ounces! Of course, if you have to imbibe an
alcoholic beverage, nibbling was also allowed *ne potus
noceat*—that is, so that the alcohol would do you no
harm.

The forty-day Lenten fast (no longer obligatory) was
undertaken in imitation of Jesus, but unlike his fast, the
modern forty days was broken into segments. No one
fasted on Sundays; and the Feast of St. Patrick—as well
as of St. Joseph in some areas—was often declared to be
exempt from fasting when it occurred in Lent (as it does
more often than not).

These Christian attitudes toward fasting reflect a
humane posture similar to the rabbinical case of the
woman who craved pork.

Clearly, religious fasting is not so much for the
purpose of learning how to appreciate food as it is to
learn how to appreciate God. The only reference to
fasting in the entire Law of Moses, Leviticus 16:29,
makes this quite clear: "On the tenth day of the seventh
month [i.e., on Yom Kippur] every one of you, whether
a native or a resident alien, shall *bow your soul* and do
no work." The underlined phrase (a literal translation) is
usually translated "mortify [or "afflict"] yourself" and
means a complete fast from food. The purpose of this
fast is to establish yourself with faith in an attitude of
humility in the presence of God, showing yourself ready
to receive his action in your life.

There are other religious purposes for fasting:
purification (as in humanistic wellness); to serve as a

sign of grief and mourning; as an accompaniment to prayerful petition; as a form of protest; and as a form of asceticism or self-denial.

In Judaism, the practice of fasting had taken an honored place among religious practices together with prayer and almsgiving. But as with many good things, fasting went sour. It gradually became little more than a formality, and more than one prophet pointed this out. The prophet Isaiah (58:3a) knew that his compatriots asked God: "Why do we fast, and you do not see it? afflict ourselves, and you take no note of it?" Isaiah's response in the name of God was:

> *Lo, on your fast days you carry out your*
> > *own pursuits,*
> > *and drive all your laborers.*
> *Yes, your fast ends in quarreling and*
> > *fighting,*
> > *striking with wicked claw. . . .*
> *This, rather, is the fasting that I wish:*
> > *releasing those bound unjustly,*
> > *untying the thongs of the yoke;*
> *Setting free the oppressed,*
> > *breaking every yoke;*
> *Sharing your bread with the hungry,*
> > *sheltering the oppressed and the homeless;*
> *Clothing the naked when you see them,*
> > *and not turning your back on your own.*
> *Then your light shall break forth like*
> > *the dawn,*
> > *and your wound shall quickly be healed.*
> *(Isaiah 58:3b-4, 6-8)*

This is a wellness thrust, for it certainly bespeaks environmental sensitivity: an awareness of and concern for fellow human beings.

Jesus preached this, too. His description of the last

judgment in Matthew 25:31-46 has certainly been inspired in part by Isaiah's observations. In fact, Matthew's last judgment scene concludes a theme begun earlier in his gospel. Jesus said that the righteousness of his followers would have to surpass the righteousness of the Pharisees (5:20), who were particularly noted for the strict and meticulous observances of prayer, fasting, and almsgiving.

Ironically, Jesus did not demand a stricter observance. In fact, he didn't encourage fasting at all: "How can wedding guests go in mourning so long as the groom is with them? When the day comes that the groom is taken away, then they will fast" (Matthew 9:15). But if you elected to fast, Jesus asked that you make it qualitatively different from the fasting of the Pharisees, that you didn't make a big show of it as they did. "See to it," said Jesus, "that you groom your hair and wash your face" (Matthew 6:17). That is, show externally the joy of living which the practice of fasting is revealing to you.

Jesus preferred that the righteousness of his followers be displayed in other kinds of deeds: works of mercy (9:13; 12:7), particularly as shown to those who are weak and are like children. Extending mercy to such is like extending it to Jesus himself (18:5).

Of course, Jesus himself fasted (Matthew 4:1-2), and he seems to have done so to insure his openness to God the Father. But the Christian Scriptures written about him and after him didn't place any special emphasis on fasting, nor did they grant it any special religious meaning (Romans 14:14-20; 1 Corinthians 10:25-26).

Yet Jesus did say to *all*: "Whoever wishes to be my follower must deny his very self, take up his cross each day, and follow in my steps. Whoever would save his life will lose it, and whoever loses his life for my sake will save it" (Luke 9:23-24). Jesus' paradoxical teaching suggests that the true meaning and pleasures of life are to be discovered through a process of mortification and self-denial. Fasting is only one small part of a much larger picture.

The larger picture is asceticism, a search for higher levels of life, consciousness, and spirituality. Fasting is just one among many elements of renunciation, self-abnegation, and sacrifice that are the stock-in-trade of this kind of asceticism. Just as humanistic wellness abstains from food to gain a certain bodily purity as well as a better appreciation for nourishment, so a Christian wellness life-style pursues fasting and other ascetical practices to develop an openness and receptivity to higher levels of life and other dimensions of human existence.

Francis of Assisi is one Christian who developed such an approach to wellness, to life's better pleasures. In his *Rule*, Francis urged his followers to adopt a life of penance (the concept involved a change of heart, a change of perspective). One aspect of this life-style was fasting. In Chapter Three of his *Rule* he asks his friars to fast during Lent and for another forty-day period extending from the Feast of All Saints to Christmas. He also urged a weekly fast on Friday.

Then Francis demonstrated a positive aspect of fasting. He proposed a voluntary forty-day beginning on the feast of the Epiphany (January 6) in honor of the forty-day fast of Jesus following his baptism in the Jordan (which tradition believed to have taken place around this time).

Further, Francis's suggestions for fasting were marked by two distinct characteristics: moderation, and an absence of detailed specificity. While he certainly desired that his followers practice fasting, Francis did add "Where there is a clear necessity, they need not do any corporal fasting." He appreciated and respected individual differences as well as other conditions (such as the nature of one's work, or one's climate) in which fasting was impractical.

In addition, Francis (unlike heads of other orders at
that time) gave no specific directions as to the manner
of fasting. Since the friars were to work for their
sustenance and had to accept what they were given,
they had to practice moderation accordingly. Beggars
could never be choosers.

In Francis' day, the translation of Mark 9:29
included the phrase "and fasting" at its conclusion:
"This kind (of demon) you can drive out only by
prayer." Reflecting on that text, Francis decided that
fasting was a key way to be delivered from the demons
of self-interest and self-centeredness. Only by dying to
self through fasting and other works of self-denial and
mortification could one become more open to God and
to higher dimensions of human life.

Actually, Francis saw at least three reasons for
pursuing a life of penance. First, he believed it would
free you from excessive focus on self and on the joys of
this life, so as to allow a taste of the joys of divine love.
In other words, Francis encouraged his followers to
discover what he himself had discovered: There is more
to life than meets the eye; there are levels of life and
experience that we fail to grasp because we choose not
to look beyond the present, earthly, flesh-bound
existence. Coming from a man who drank deeply of
life's pleasures before his conversion, these comments are
intriguing and encouraging. Francis experienced what
many wellness educators encourage: a widening of
horizons and human sensitivity to the life of the spirit.
For Francis, this was an experience of God himself.

A second reason for mortification and self-denial
was to remove any impediments to God's action in us,
so that we might be more open to his will and designs.
Properly understood, Francis' advice is not to resign
from self-responsibility and self-determination, but rather
to sharpen perspective and understanding so as to begin
to see meaning in the apparently senseless experiences of

life. For a person who views God as the meaning and purpose and pleasure of human life, all things and all experiences do converge to well-being: People, things, and circumstances, no matter who or what they may be, contribute to the overall meaning of life. Modern Christian spirituality calls this discernment.

A third reason for the life of penance suggested by Francis to his followers is not for the sanctification and welfare of the individual but for the good of the Kingdom, for the benefit of others who would like to submit to the reign of God. Francis urged his followers to pursue the virtue of "minority," the virtue of being little, for the purpose of bringing forth fruit *in* the Church. Notice he said *in* and not *for* the Church. The point is that his followers were to be catalytic and were not to aspire to positions of dominance. Francis felt that so long as his followers remained at the grass-roots level with the troops, they could be of best service to others.

This last point suggests that the Christian wellness life-style may be able to surpass the basic wellness approach on a fundamental point: self. There may be a risk in wellness that the individual can become self-centered and rather unconcerned about others. The Christian perspective, especially as urged by Francis for his followers, is *not* that they do wellness for others but rather that they continue to witness to and educate for ever-higher levels of wellness. "Blessed is the man," said Francis, "who bears with his neighbor in his weakness so much as he would wish to be treated by him were he in a like situation" (*Admonition*, n. 18). This may sound like the golden rule, but it is far different. The motive is not reciprocity but rather the experienced love of Jesus and the riches of the life to which all believers are called.

Not only did Francis urge restraint in imposing ideas upon others, but he urged his friars to be moderate in their own ascetical practices as they pursued ever-higher levels of wellness. His biographer, Thomas of Celano, notes: "He told the friars that every offering made to God was to be seasoned with salt (Leviticus 2:13), and warned that each must consider his own physical capacity in honoring God. It was just as much a sin, he asserted, to deny indiscreetly what the body needed as it was to fall into gluttony and give the body more than was needful" (2 Celano, n. 22).

Recent scientific examination of his exhumed bones indicated that Francis suffered from malnutrition. By twentieth-century standards Francis may indeed have damaged his health, but by the standards of the thirteenth century in which he lived, he made prudential judgments on his own behalf and allowed his followers the same option. Judging from his writings and the writings of his many followers through the centuries, a wide variety of life-styles is possible, each of which leads in its own way to some very high levels of wellness, to genuinely purposeful and immeasurably pleasurable life.

When on his deathbed he was told he had lived too strict a life, Francis accepted the judgment. "Rejoice, Brother Body," he said, "and spare me, because I now gladly do what you wish and hasten to fulfill your complaints and desires" (2 Celano, n. 211). The asceticism of Francis was impressively free from rigidity and obstinate attachment to self-determined goals. His primary goal was to seek for the best way to allow God to act unhindered in the heart of an individual. Any advice that would contribute to that was always most welcome.

CONCLUSION

Life indeed is a banquet, and wellness invites more and more people to come and take their fair share. Humanistic wellness educators urge you to reflect on the meaning and purpose of life, as well as the meaning of many activities that sustain and promote life: nutritional awareness, physical fitness, control of stress, environmental sensitivity, and self-responsibility. The aim is to help you once more discover the true joys of living and the pleasures that can be enhanced by a wellness life-style.

The Jew has always emphasized the joy of living and has freely shared that joy with others. (Think, for example, of the many Jewish comedians who draw incredible amounts of their material from their religious literature and traditions!) Though I focused on food and eating as one way to appreciate the Jewish zest for life, this is by no means a narrow focus. The rabbis believe that dietetics not only refers to nutrition, as our modern word denotes, but also covers the total life-style of a person: residence, clothing, sports, work, and many other items. Their discussions are eloquent testimony to the potential fullness of this life and the countless joys that can be found in it.

The Christian perspective on life shares this Jewish outlook, though Christianity has developed an aspect that is complementary: fasting. Of course, fasting is not unique to Christianity, but its purpose and meaning in Christianity is.

Christians have a high degree of interest in what they call the spiritual life, the richer dimensions of human life possible already here on earth and available to anyone who wants to pursue them. Jesus repeatedly pointed to these dimensions in his teaching and preaching. Francis of Assisi, that faithful mirror of the life of Jesus, accepted the suggestions of Jesus and urged his followers to do likewise as they sought ever-higher levels of wellness, especially the ineffable pleasures to be derived from the life of the spirit. The Christian pattern is to seek these levels through asceticism: self-denial, mortification, and similar practices.

Both of these approaches to the banquet of life are good: One is life-affirming, the other seems world-denying. The Catholic theologian Karl Rahner, however, warns against retaining a too-rigid separation between the two. "God is greater than our heart," he says. "An empty heart does not force him to come down, and a heart filled with the splendour of God's creation does not by that alone already possess the true God."[4] Each person must decide for herself or himself the concrete measure of asceticism and world-affirmation that will make for the personally appropriate life-style that will clearly lead to ever-higher levels of wellness, to the fullness of life's pleasures.

Some ethnic Christian customs appear to have struck the balance Rahner describes.

The traditional Polish Christmas Eve dinner is one example. In the old calenders the day was one of fast (one full meal) and abstinence (no meat). The meal, therefore, was mainly dairy products and fish, but it was tasty in true peasant fashion.

The table was covered with a clean white table-cloth, and each plate was set upon some straw, reminiscent of Jesus' first bedding. The meal did not begin until the youngest child observed the first star in the sky and came inside to tell the family.

Before sitting down to eat, each member of the family, beginning with the parents and including all the children, shared *opłatek* (that is, broke bread) with other members, begging pardon for injuries of the preceding year, promising to improve loving relations, and wishing well for the coming year.

The meal varied between nine and twelve or more courses, depending on the traditions cherished by the family. It was concluded with the singing of some of the theologically rich *koledy* (carols), sometimes lasting until the time for midnight Mass.

The masterfully blended life-affirming and

69529

world-denying dimensions of a high-level wellness life-style captured in this tradition show that you really can enjoy the best of both worlds, or can have your cake and eat it too, as you design your own wellness life-style. In the next chapter I will point to the potential at every stage of life, from womb to tomb. But before moving to the next chapter, you might wish to turn to the reflection questions at the end of the book, especially those on life's pleasures, joys, satisfactions. You might want to focus on other aspects of joy and pleasure in life, such as intellectual pursuits, sex, music, and dance.

NOTES

1. I have not seen the final report from that 1977 survey, but a related article treating both these insights is Nancy Milio, Ph.D., R.N., "A Framework for Prevention: Changing Health-Damaging to Health-Generating Life Patterns," *American Journal of Public Health*, 66 (1976): 435-39.

2. Robert Farrar Capon, *The Supper of the Lamb* (Garden City, New York: Doubleday & Co., Inc., 1969). Father Capon might be distressed to see me include his insights in the section of the chapter entitled "Humanistic Perspectives." I know his faith as it shines through his writings; but I find his insights and presentations so suitable in discussions with my humanist friends that I felt it would be quite appropriate to include them here. Capon serves on the editorial board of *Body & Soul*, a spirituality newsletter very compatible with a wellness spirituality. Readers can request a sample from Alchemy Communications, P.O. Box 257, Oregon, IL 61061.

3. This insight is phrased "not after death life, but out of death life" in "Jesus: Key to the Abundant Life," *Sisters Today*, 46 (April 1975): 462-572. The theme developed in the section of the chapter is further developed in module three, "Life's Pleasures" in the program, *Developing an Holistic Spirituality* (Sewanee, Tenn.: The University of the South, 1980). Yet another development from other biblical texts can be heard in the cassette "The Pleasures of Life," in *Parish Wellness: Renewal for the 1980's* (Kansas City, Mo.: NCR Cassettes, 1980).

4. Karl Rahner, "The Passion and Asceticism: Thoughts on the Philosophical-theological Basis of Christian Asceticism," in *Theological Investigations*, Vol. III (Baltimore: Helicon Press, 1967), p. 81.

CHAPTER FIVE

LIFELONG WELLNESS

In my understanding of wellness, freedom of self-determination is the core, the heart of the matter. "You alone do it," I continue to repeat, yet always hasten to add "*but* you don't do it alone." In other words, wellness is freely self-conceived, self-initiated, self-fulfilled, or self-"messed-up." The person pursuing a wellness life-style can never say, "The Devil made me do it" or "God made me do it" or "My mother/father made me do it." In wellness, the individual can take all the credit and all the blame.

"*But* you don't do it alone" adds the obvious. We live—most of us, at any rate—in society. We need the help, the cooperation of others, and we have an effect on others. This consideration does indeed temper freedom of self-responsibility for some. It doesn't faze others. The point is that wellness is not something that can be ingested in a pill or forced upon a person by an expert or by some other authority. God created Adam and Eve with freedom to such an extent that they were entirely able to disobey, to go their own way. And Jesus similarly left the choice of following him up to the freedom of those invited. Some (the Twelve) did; others (the rich aristocrat, Nicodemus) didn't. Each one determines his or her own level of wellness and the path along which to pursue it.

Life, however, is understood differently at different ages. The six-year-old and sixty-year-old make different choices because they understand life differently. At ages eighteen, forty, and sixty, even the same set of alternatives will probably elicit different choices. If, as I insist, wellness hinges on freedom of self-determination, then wellness depends upon how we make life's major decisions and how we live with the consequences. Life-stage researchers have studied these decisions and their consequences and have organized their reports around their discoveries.

The work of John G. Bruhn, Ph.D., Associate Dean of Medicine at the University of Texas Medical Branch, Galveston, Texas, and that of his colleagues, for example, has done just that, and it is outstanding from the purely humanistic perspective.[1] Very briefly, what they have done is superimposed their understanding of wellness on Erik Erikson's stages of development and correlated the developmental tasks identified by Robert Havighurst. Their models and charts are quite complete and clear. In this section of this chapter, I summarize their model and suggest points at which Jewish and Christian spiritual values and religious beliefs might be relevant. Those interested in a purely humanistic approach will probably find the recent work of Annette Hollander, M.D., as useful as I have in public speeches.[2]

WELLNESS PRIOR TO SELF-DETERMINATION

Opinions vary about the precise point in an individual's life at which true, free self-determination actually takes place. The commonly accepted view among Catholics, for instance—that at some point around seven years of age one reaches the age of reason and with it the ability to seriously offend God—also recognizes that at age seven most children are subject to a variety of authorities: parents, school, the state, and others, all of whom have rules or laws that restrict freedom of self-determination. The life-stages researchers have noted that it is probably somewhere between adolescence and adulthood (no one assigns a definite number to that age) that a person can first make a truly free decision. That person can say, "Thanks, but I won't register for the selective service system"; or "Thanks, but I don't want to belong to this religion in which you've reared me since youth, and I'm quitting right now"; or "Thanks, but I refuse to wear a helmet when I ride my motorcycle."

Thus, Bruhn and his colleagues propose a distinction which I've adopted in this chapter: between wellness prior to self-determination and wellness after self-determination. Prior to self-determination others (adults: especially parents, teachers, neighbors, clergy) give a maximum of effort and attention to the basic needs of the individual. In other words, at this time of life "adult others" play the most significant role; self plays a lesser role. This usually changes after one reaches self-determination.

What is possible, desirable, and necessary is that the young person experience wellness models in day-to-day living and experience responsible loving care from others. These models ought to reflect various approaches to life, various life-styles based on a wide variety of different philosophical, religious, or spiritual viewpoints. Such an experience in youth contributes to a wellness-readiness. Bruhn's model and explanations will serve as the vehicle for this section's development. Adult readers should ask what they can do to function as models or guides for youngsters in each step along the way to their self-determination.

Infancy (Trust)
During infancy the child should experience a protective environment, with attentive and caring models who fulfill physical, social, psychological, and spiritual needs. This is when the child learns trust and becomes aware of how to fulfill needs. The young person also senses how these needs and their fulfillment are valued by others.

It is essential at this point in life that the person experience continuity of care in contrast to episodic care, so that a good foundation for wellness will be laid. If a child's diapers are not changed as often as necessary, this episodic care teaches the child to consider cleanliness as not very necessary or desirable. But undiscriminating continuous care can be just as damaging. If a child's every cry (attention-getting, pain-expressing, hunger, diaper-change, and so on) is met with a feeding, the child intuits that the solution to every problem is eating, a solution that can lead to weight problems in later life.

From the spiritual and religious perspective, continuity of care is also highly prized. Judaism practices infant circumcision of boys, and most Christians retain infant Baptism for boys and girls. In keeping with modern sensitivity to the dignity and rights of women, some Jews have devised ceremonies for naming infant girls. One such ceremony is called the *berit* of candles and is based on Deuteronomy 29:9-14, where women are given a recognized role in the covenant. At least part of the reason why both religious traditions observe these practices is to impress upon children that religion and spirituality are important wellness dimensions of adult life, and caring parents (and other adults) want to communicate that message to their offspring as early in life as possible. Both traditions will offer the children an opportunity to reaffirm or reject this element later in life.

Early Childhood (Autonomy)
Soon enough the child begins to attempt things on personal initiative. The young person begins to take risks and learns to accept all outcomes, good and bad, rewards and punishments. In the process there is an opportunity to learn the consequences of one's own actions and of the actions of others.

Adult models are keenly important at this stage, since the child has no concept of health but only imitates what is experienced. Parents guide the learning of basic skills and individual responsibility. It is imperative for them to pursue and practice health and wellness life-styles for children to witness and aspire to. And it is damaging, on the other hand, for parents and other adults to say, "Do as I say, not as I do."[3] It must be confusing to youth to see athletic heroes promote beer on television commercials, or to read that athletic heroes die from lung cancer caused by smoking tobacco.

Studies indicate that warm and nurturant home environments where parents are in control and where they urge high-maturity responses while avoiding authoritarian discipline contribute to the development of a sense of belonging, an extroverted personality, and qualities such as competence, independence and self-control—all of which result from independent decision-making in the family circle. Granted, much of what is learned at this stage makes little immediate sense. But its relevance (or irrelevance) will be judged at a later stage in life.

Religion and spirituality also make contributions to the sense of autonomy, the sense of community, and the importance of reconciliation. Harry Golden, former editor of the *Carolina Israelite*, tells of learning the spirit

of prayer and the nature of God from his mother. She
was always dialoguing aloud with God, her silent and
invisible companion. To God she made many comments
about Harry's decisions, choices, and activities, always
within his earshot. What he didn't understand at that
time, he learned to appreciate later in life.

Christians, too, like to teach prayer to children at a
tender age and model it by praying with them at
mealtime, bedtime, and other times. Christians believe
that the spirit of prayer is an early entrée into exploring
the purpose and meaning of life and the place and role
of God in human existence. Both the Jewish and the
Christian traditions view childhood as an important
time for adults to teach children the responsibility that
must accompany autonomy.

Youngsters are also introduced to some ritual
aspects of religion at this period. The ritual celebration
of the Jewish Passover meal requires the youngest of
those present to ask questions of the person presiding so
that the tradition might be explained. If the youngest
person is a child too young to ask, he or she ought to
be prompted to do so. In any event, the explanation is
paramount and cannot be omitted.

Christian children are invited to participate in
eucharistic celebrations and to share in the Lord's
Supper at an early age. While the Eucharist is not fully
appreciated at this stage, it is believed that continued
faithful participation will ultimately lead the young
believer to a fuller comprehension of the mystery.
Again, both traditions see such rituals as an important
element introducing the youngster to the community
which forms the family's spiritual heritage, as well as
introducing the child to the role of this religious
community as an extension of the family (for instance,
in the Christian notion of godparents or sponsors), as a
caring group, and as a support system in life.

In the Catholic tradition, this is also a time of

preparation for the reception of the sacrament of
Penance as the young person comes to realize more
consciously that some actions displease other people and
even disrupt a relationship to the extent that a
reconciliation is required. Learned in the family circle
and reinforced in the religious community, the practice
and spirit of reconciliation is a valuable component of a
wellness life-style to which religion can add a uniquely
sensitive dimension. (As a youngster I was instructed in
school to seek out each family member I had offended
and apologize before leaving for the customary Saturday
afternoon "confession" at church.)

Late Childhood (Initiative)
A positive self-concept, the development of good feelings
about every aspect of one's life, is a key element of
wellness that can be learned at this stage. Studies show
that persons with a high degree of self-esteem are the
most likely to initiate preventive measures in their
health styles and to faithfully maintain them ever after.
The successful and satisfying learning of social trust and
autonomy at early stages of growth lays the solid
foundation upon which the individual can begin to take
initiative, to take risks.

Rules and carefully defined standards and limits on
the behavior of youth are necessary in this period, but
so too is a concern for understanding children's views,
respecting their opinions, and granting concessions as
necessary. A positive perspective is much more desirable
than a list of prohibitions. It is better to explain how a
rule or practice enhances life and its joy rather than
how its transgression causes damage: "Breathe clean air
and you'll feel more energetic" rather than "Don't
smoke tobacco, or you'll get cancer."

Academic and intellectual skills also begin to
develop at this stage, but it is unfortunate that so much
education (whether health, wellness, or religious) aims at

promoting docility rather than encouraging intellectual curiosity, self-expression, and sensitivity to differing values. Wellness is rooted in these latter values, not in docility.

This is also the period in which the young person can begin to develop a functional concept of health and in which the foundation for wellness can be laid, but the tug of war among home, school, church, and society about who should teach what hardly helps.

Consider sex education for youngsters. Everyone agrees that it is important, but agreement stops right there. Parents and other adults with an undeveloped or underdeveloped wellness life-style generally will allow no one else to handle the matter, but they often fail to do it themselves. Schools that fear displeasing such parents are then reduced to problem-and-crisis-centered health education such as the risks of venereal disease and the hazards of teen-age pregnancies (currently of epidemic proportions in the United States).

Some churches contribute their obstacle by treating sex as something suspect, a source of temptation, a stumbling block to holiness. Church teachings and attitudes toward the body (particularly as contrasted with concern for saving the soul) unwittingly but effectively lessen the sense of self-esteem a person might have. Comedian George Carlin's routine on impure thoughts, words, and deeds is funny because it is at least partly true even today. One theologian parodied Christian sexual teaching of the past thus: "Sex is dirty. Save it for someone you love!"

Granted, Christian education has moved toward improving this dimension of its subject matter. But there is still much it can learn from its Jewish heritage, which *The Second Jewish Catalogue* sums up thus:

> Human sexuality, like every human capacity, comes from God and is therefore holy and good—provided

that it is exercised in faithful acceptance of God's purpose and in reverent awareness of His presence. The proper sexual relation is that which serves both to express and to further, on an enduring basis, the mutually responsive and responsible love of a man and woman who recognize that each has been created in God's image.[4]

I remember hearing a rabbi discuss this topic in a public lecture. He reminded the audience of the Adam and Eve story. He said the Talmud noted that it wasn't until Adam and Eve were expelled from the garden that Eve became pregnant. From this, the rabbis concluded that the primary purpose of sex in marriage was pleasure (which is what Adam and Eve must have been sharing prior to the expulsion), and the secondary purpose of marriage was procreation. Recent Christian teaching on the purpose of sex in marriage has come closer to this Jewish position, although it no longer rank-orders the purposes.[5] Such an outlook can lead to a healthy, wholesome, and vibrant understanding of life's genuine purpose and fulfilling pleasure.

In both traditions, this stage leads to rites of puberty: *Bar/Bat miṣwah* and Confirmation. These rites are important, since these events coincide with the basic—perhaps for the first time truly free—decision for or against a wellness life-style.

Early Adolescence (Industry)
This stage, according to Erikson, is the most socially decisive for the growing person. It is the time when the individual begins to sense unique identity and begins to develop attitudes toward work. It is critically important that adults avoid creating the impression that personal identity and worth are defined and determined by your job. It is sad indeed if the young person encounters only models of the unreflectively accepted work ethic which

holds that the sole purpose in life is survival. Such models only reinforce what the youngster begins to believe: All that counts is living from day to day.

Here is a precious opportunity for helping the young person to consider work and career choices in the wellness context as well as in the economic context. The early adolescent should be encouraged to consider the contrast of what others consider important and worthy of reward with what he or she consider important. Perhaps there is no reward, or no adequate reward, for his or her main interest in life. Perhaps negative aspects of a career outweigh positive aspects, thus suggesting an alternative choice that may be economically less appealing. Wellness may not rank particularly high in the growing personal value system of early adolescents, but young people need to be exposed to it as a value so that it can be included when future plans are being considered. Using the reflection guides at the end of this book will help you explore the meaning and purpose of your own life and of your job; it will likewise encourage youngsters to consider how and why they make one career choice and not another.

At this stage the individual begins to develop a philosophy of life and needs very much to be open to the widest horizons of human potential. Both the Jewish *Bar/Bat miṣwah* and the Confirmation preparations in the Jewish and Christian traditions can make major contributions to this element in the wellness life-style. If religious instruction in each instance is keyed closer to the realities of daily life experiences of the young person, it will have greater impact on later wellness decisions open to the youngsters.[6] This period is the threshold of self-determination.[7]

SELF-DETERMINATION: DECIDING FOR (OR AGAINST) WELLNESS

Up to this point in human growth and development, the youngster has only observed wellness or sickness models (mainly parents and other adults in the family setting). Not yet having the power of free self-determination, he or she has little or no capability of personally selecting a wellness-conducive, health-conducive, or sickness-conducive life-style. The largest burden until now rests upon parents and other elders to be certain that they have shared good wellness information and provided persuasive models of wellness for youngsters to observe and aspire to emulate.

But beginning with adolescence, or more accurately at some point between adolescence and young adulthood (no one is willing to identify that point with a specific age), the individual becomes capable of making and actually does make a truly free decision. And the nature of the decisions changes, too. For at this time of life the decisions are of greater importance. It is no longer a question of deciding which dress or tie to wear, but rather what to do with one or another dimension of one's life: for example, school, career, job, marriage.

Bruhn's schema continues into this part of life as well, and it is very good. But I have found the work of adult life-stages researchers, such as Daniel Levinson,[8] Penelope Washbourn (who is primarily a theologian)[9], and Gail Sheehy[10] even more useful to wellness discussions.[11] The themes discussed by Levinson and Washbourn are nearly identical with the themes of my wellness definition: life's meaning and joys, life's purpose and satisfaction, choices and freedom of self-determination, responsibility for initiative, living with consequences of choice, changing, etc.

In this section I will continue briefly along the lines of Bruhn's model (adolescence) but then fashion my consideration after Levinson's schema (young, middle, late adulthood). You are encouraged, while reading this chapter, to consult the reflection questions (at the end of the book) that are keyed to this chapter.

Adolescence (Identity)
At adolescence the individual starts shaping his or her
own identity and begins to select appropriate values
while discarding others. The adolescent will compare the
values learned at home with values promoted by society
at large. If health-damaging practices have been valued
at home, society's encouragement of health-hazardous
behavior will meet no resistance in the adolescent.
Social expectation rather than personal conviction
independently achieved will dominate his or her choices.
Unfortunately, society downplays the dangers of the
risks by encouraging two basic beliefs: That can't
happen to me; but if it does, medical science will have
discovered a cure or remedy by that time. Youth's
general feeling of physical indestructibility, for example,
strengthens these beliefs. The same could be said for
youth's attitudes toward the possiblity of a less-than-
happy choice of spouse, career, or whatever. It won't
happen to me; if it does, someone can fix it.

Both Judaism and Christianity, as well as
humanistic philosophies, teach moderation, self-restraint,
and even self-denial. Indeed, some people believe that
the Christian Scriptures are clearly counter-cultural
challenges, and Judaism's concern about being holy also
raises many a question about society's operational
principles. If these elements of the tradition have
received adequate emphasis in the formative years, the
adolescent will have no difficulty continuing them as
difficult wellness decisions begin to occur. On the other
hand, if wellness has not been viewed as a value earlier
in life, it will be difficult if not impossible to make a
beginning now.

Wellness is defined by each individual, uniquely
and quite personally. Success, happiness, career and job
satisfaction are too often social definitions. (Consider for
a moment how you have answered the reflection
questions at the end of this book.) To formulate a

personal philosophy of wellness and to live by its principles will demand strength and courage to stand up firmly against suggestions to live less effectively. It is difficult to live contrary to the conventionally accepted behavior in society, but wellness sometimes demands nothing less. Adolescents in particular may find such a suggestion unreasonable, since their experience leads them to believe, for example, that they are indestructible and their ideas are perfect. Their bodies, for example, rebound so quickly and resiliently from life-style excesses that it is difficult for them to believe there could be lasting physical or even mental damage from such a life-style.

A final delusion of this period is the belief that choices made now last forever. The common phrase "getting your act together" intimates that once this is done the "act" stays together for life. While this is entirely possible and probable, it is wise to consider that wellness requires constant openness to new choices. Wellness may require that you change your job, change your living location, change your vocation, and perhaps make other sad but necessary changes. Resistance to change, or the inability to make necessary changes, is an impediment to wellness. Wellness is a lifelong process, but its personal initiation begins in adolescence.

Early or Young Adulthood (Intimacy)
Erikson notes that once identity has been established, a person is prepared to seek intimacy with others. From the wellness perspective, the range of choices offered by society at this point in the life-cycle and the relationship of those choices to developing intimacy are particularly important. Unfortunately, intimacy may suffer as a consequence of the other choices clamoring for personal attention.

Though it is important earlier in life, it seems even more important at this time to respect the very real

differences between men and women. Levinson's work
was based on his study of men and is intended chiefly
for men. He admits it may have some applicability to
women, but he insists that similar research must be
carried out by women with women subjects. For this
reason I have turned to Washbourn's book. It is clearly
autobiographical and shows familiarity with and
reference to other research, and thus it is not exactly a
parallel to Levinson's work. But I found Washbourn's
book much more useful to me than Sheehy's, chiefly
because Washbourn's insights did not seem to raise the
wrath of women in my audiences as much as Sheehy's
did and because Washbourn's viewpoints meshed neatly
with my wellness notions. (Perhaps the fact that we are
both primarily theologians explains the compatibility of
our ideas.)

In any case, wellness in early or young adulthood
depends on how we make the major decisions at this
time and on how we proceed to live with the
consequences of those decisions. Adapting Levinson to
my religious/spiritual perspectives, I have rephrased
these major decisions this way:
1. Forming a dream;
2. forming a mentor relationship;
3. forming an occupation/ministry;
4. forming a vocation/state in life.

The dream hinges on a number of variables, and
the individual person must strive to sort them out. In
the past, boys and girls grew up to be young men and
young women with different dreams. Sheehy's listing of
women's life-patterns that resulted from the choices
society allowed, ranging from the more traditional to the
experimental, invites the reader to compare a personal
dream to what Sheehy discovered in her interviews:[12]
1. Caregiver—a woman who marries young (early
twenties or younger) and gives no thought at the
time to ever moving beyond a domestic role.

2. Either/or—a woman in her twenties who either nurtures and defers achievement or who achieves and defers nurturing. Both are good choices. An interesting side question not raised by Sheehy is the effect of the latter choice upon a spouse of low-level wellness whose masculinity or masculine fulfillment is apparently thereby threatened.

3. Integrator—one who chooses to combine marriage, career, and motherhood. Sheehy notes, however, that this choice is practically impossible at 20, quite possible at 30, and most definitely possible at 35. Women physicians and former members of women's religious communities provide some unanticipated confirmation of Sheehy's hunches.

4. Never-married woman—one who chooses to "marry" a job, a community project, or something else which provides pseudo-family relationships and obligations.

5. Transient—a woman who chooses impermanence as a life-style.

Did women dream these choices? Can they change the dream? Are they willing to? Answers to these and similar questions begin to put you on the path to defining or redefining your personal wellness.

A mentor or an advisor is someone who relates to the dream in some fashion. Men might find a "patron" within the corporate structure who helps pave the way to success; women might find someone to assist in breaking down sexist barriers and moving their dream closer to fulfillment. The mentor can be of either sex for either sex. It would also seem that the mentor could be of any age, and not necessarily fall in the rigid age classifications posed by Levinson.

While most researchers speak of forming an occupation, I've modified that to include forming a ministry. Occupation is so strongly linked with the idea of a job that it doesn't seem to include the possible consideration of doing something for nothing, as some forms of ministry do. Including the word *ministry* (sometimes used to translate the Greek *diakonia*, service) in one of the major choices of life also broadens the horizons for occupations. Can medicine be a ministry? Is it impossible to combine job and ministry? What is the significance of the increasing popularity of hyphenated occupations: e.g., full-time elementary teacher/part-time opera singer? How were or are your choices of occupation/ministry affected by such factors as parental values, guidance counselors, concern for salary, or desire to "make it"?

Finally, I've broadened Levinson's fourth major choice from "Forming a marriage and family" to "forming a vocation/state in life." Not everyone gets married; some people are satisfied to remain single. Some dedicate their lives to the medical missions or to religious communities, for example. I believe that in his research Levinson wasn't concerned with marriage so much as with the question of whether individuals had ample opportunity to form adult peer relationships with the opposite sex. In the United States, marriage used to take place at an early age, even before the individuals had time to learn how to develop highly loving, sexually free, and emotionally intimate relationships. Thus, when Levinson speaks of "forming" a marriage he refers to the effort required to develop the relationships just mentioned. This would appear to be the same kind of task Erikson has in mind when he discusses the challenge of developing intimacy in this period of life.

Penelope Washbourn comments appropriately from a woman's perspective: "The graceful experience of sexuality involves a perception that a woman's identity cannot be located *exclusively* in being loved, in being able to bear children, or in being a wife or a mother."[13]

In short, according to Erikson, wellness in early or

young adulthood requires the personal development of
intimacy in all persons; according to Levinson, it
requires that men successfully complete the four major
tasks facing them; according to Washbourn, it requires
that women make a personally graceful (life-affirming,
growth-promoting) response to the challenges peculiar to
women at this time of life.

I often think of Jesus as a representative inhabitant
of a Mediterranean country: an adult Jewish male of
marriageable age who was unmarried, who associated for
the most part with twelve men, seemed to have no job,
and went around chewing the fat with the folks. I
wonder if his mother ever said: "For the love of God,
think of me and what the neighbors are saying. Get a
job! Get married!" Or did she recognize his happiness
and satisfaction with that life-style, a high-level wellness
life-style (to retroject our concept some twenty centuries)?
The same could be said for the great prophets in Judaism
like Jeremiah, who remained unmarried, and Ezekiel, who
did not grieve the loss of his wife, because they believed
that God had shown them a different and more fulfilling
purpose and pleasure in life. And all three of these
religious figures give evidence of a rich capability for
intimacy, developed in a life-situation that was different
from the ordinary life-styles of their peers. (The reader
might want to pause at this point and turn to the
reflection questions on young adulthood.)

Middle Adulthood (Generativity)
While up until now the person has been a learner, this
stage of life marks a turning point: He or she wants to
become a teacher. Each individual begins to wonder
what is most important about life and living that is
worth passing on to the next generation. Generativity,
as Erikson understands it, is not simply productivity
(such as leaving behind a monument or memorial),
creativity (such as giving humankind a new invention),

or having children (perpetuating yourself), but something much more. It includes sharing with the younger generation *your* philosophical and spiritual tradition, your understanding of wellness.

At this stage in life the challenge to wellness involves some stock-taking. Undoubtedly one part of the philosophical tradition Americans want to pass on to the next generation is that hard work and persistence are the key to success. It also intimates, even if it doesn't explicitly state, that health and well-being are acceptable sacrifices for achieving success. You can take pride in becoming the foreman, chief operator, or executive director, even if that position has afflicted you with high blood pressure which daily threatens you with a stroke or kidney damage. Ironically, it is just such a temporary or permanent loss of health at this stage that prompts a person to review her or his philosophy of life, her or his understanding of wellness.

Levinson agrees with Erikson in noting that the opposite of generativity is stagnation. Levinson says it is imperative to experience stagnation if you want to achieve generativity. A person has to "have the sense of not growing, of being static, stuck, drying up, bogged down in a life-full of obligation and devoid of self-fulfillment. He must know the experience of dying, of living in the shadow of death."[14]

I find this amazingly similar to what Jews would call the Exodus experience or the Passover experience, and what Christians recognize as the Paschal mystery: not "after death, life," but "out of death, life"! (See pages 43-44.) In other words, if each of these religious traditions has taught its heritage well, the believer has at hand a ready tool for understanding his or her life experience and a reliable means of reaching for the next level of wellness. To have misunderstood the tradition as simple perseverance in adversity, sticking it out, offering it up and the like, is to miss the chance for wellness.

Timing would also seem to be of essence. A recent state-wide survey in Wisconsin revealed that unemployed men 44 years old and older were mentally healthier than their employed peers! Yet unemployed men 35 to 43 years of age exhibited the poorest mental health of all surveyed.

This seems to fit well with the results of life-stage study. Age 35 to 43 for a man is the period of mid-life explosion. It is the time of middle adulthood, when a man has to make it or break it. It's go for broke. To be unemployed then is a personal disaster.

But the next age cohort, 44 and older, is a settling-down period of life where money is not as important a consideration as it has been. The unemployed 44-year-old men in the survey were mentally healthier because they no longer defined their worth and identity exclusively or even mainly in terms of their jobs. Life means more than that, and to realize it is to have attained a respectable level of wellness.

Levinson also singles out four basic polarities that are present in all of life, but which surface here in a man's life for him to reexamine and rebalance as needed. The polarities are young/old, destruction/creation, masculine/feminine, and attachment/separateness.[15] The man now must face aging, the gradual diminishing of strength and other qualities that flourish in youth, and must make appropriate adjustments.

Similarly, the man in mid-life or middle-adulthood who has made a "hit" list consisting of those who have in some way hurt him earlier in life, for instance by thwarting a career plan or an important life choice, must come to terms with his anger and destructive tendency and try to channel that energy into a creative movement.

Perhaps the greatest challenge at this time of life for a man is to learn how to become masculinely feminine, and for a woman to learn how to become femininely masculine. It is time to seek to understand those traits, talents, or skills which we men have identified chiefly with the opposite sex and to try to realize that they can enrich our own personal life as well. In the United States this may be especially hard for men, but the researchers indicate that it is a truly enriching experience when it is accepted rather than rejected.

Finally, it is important for the man to rebalance attachment and separateness. After a long period of "joining" and "belonging" (lodges, clubs, professional associations, e.g.), he needs to learn how to seek, find, and relish separateness, quiet time, being alone. This balance is important for women as well. For it is in separateness that two healthy and necessary forms of fantasy and imagination can grow and develop: meditation and reverie. After a lengthy period of striving for mastery and achievement, now is a good time for passivity as in passive prayer or mystical prayer.

Again speaking about some women, Washbourn appropriately remarks: "The woman who has found her identity *exclusively* in mothering faces the crises of middle-life with the least resources."[16] And still later she notes:

> The paradox of woman's attempt to live up to the traditional image of the mother or wife who gives her life for her children is that above all she has neglected her personal and spiritual development. Women who have been cheated of an opportunity to develop themselves in the intellect or the artistic spirit find themselves most severely handicapped in old age.[17]

To summarize, the wellness challenge in middle adulthood is to refine and further develop generativity (Erikson) in order, among other reasons, to leave a legacy (Levinson). To develop generativity to the utmost requires a rebalancing of basic polarities: youth/old age; destructiveness/creativity; masculinity/femininity; and attachment/separateness (Levinson). Women, too, must make a graceful response to these and similar challenges in their lives (Washbourn).

At this point, see the reflection questions relevant to middle adulthood. Match your experiences with my development here in the text.

Late Adulthood (Ego-Integrity)
Erikson identifies ego-integrity as the final stage of human development. Ego-integrity has many things in common with wellness: It results from a process, it emphasizes individual uniqueness, and it requires self-responsibility and active personal effort.

But there is a major and significant difference between maturity and wellness. Wellness never ceases: It is an ever-expanding experience, always subject to further evaluation and improvement. Maturity is a quality attributed to an individual for acting and behaving in a certain approved fashion. A mature person may not necessarily be an adherent of a wellness life-style nor even have achieved wellness at all.

Alfred McBride suggests two characteristics of this life-stage that would most certainly fit into a wellness life-style: wisdom, and holiness.[18] The Latin word for wisdom, *sapientia*, derives from the word that means taste. Wisdom suggests a taste for living. Wise persons in late adulthood don't just know *about* life. They have drunk deeply and tasted its bitterness and sweetness better than most persons. This kind of lived and reflexive wisdom produces a discriminating judgment and gives a person a feel for what is authentic and life-affirming.

Wise elders are characterized by mellowness. They have learned to accept themselves, and this allows them

to affirm life loudly and strongly. They are also very
tolerant. Here, in fact, is the rich beauty of wise elders.
As those in our midst with the fewest years to look
forward to, they have the freedom to live life to its
fullest. And they are eager to share their wisdom with
anyone who cares to listen and to imitate their freedom.
If there were some way in our society to put youth more
closely in touch with the experience of that freedom,
wellness would have easier acceptance.

Holiness in late adulthood is not an otherworldly
characteristic but rather implies the ability of
consecrating this world. People in late adulthood who
have also achieved a good level of wellness own a
unique capacity to uncover the religious depth of life
around them. They do this with a very simple,
spontaneous, and un-self-conscious witnessing. Such
persons are endowed with a gift of pointing to the best
in life, of showing new paths to the experience of God
so effortlessly that they appear at times to be like
enchanters weaving a spell.

Once again, if religious traditions have taught
believers well their practices of prayer and meditation,
persons who have been faithful to those practices can
look to ever-richer experiences in late adulthood. They
may not have loud and booming voices any more, but
their message is no less audible.

Erikson and Levinson both affirm that this stage of
life relates back to the first stage. Erikson urges that ego-
integrity, maturity, be related back to infantile trust.
Youngsters will not fear life if elders show no fear of
death. Levinson adds that a person in late adulthood
will continue to grow and develop as long as she or he
retains a connection to youthful vitality, to the forces of
growth in self and in the world. (That is why some
nursing-home administrators view the presence of young
children in the nursing home as very beneficial to the
health and well-being of the residents.) The trick is to

retain youthfulness in a form appropriate to late adulthood.

Those who have attained this age and who also have developed a high-level wellness life-style constitute a rich resource in all our communities. There is a gathering of sages and saints who are yet to be heard from and listened to. Theirs is a rich reservoir of wisdom and spirituality whose collective voices could set a pace for our post-industrial society that would make life a lot less distressful and much more conducive to higher levels of wellness. Perhaps we have been looking too long in the wrong direction for the beautiful people.[19]

CONCLUSION

In the last analysis, lifelong wellness depends very much upon well adults. Children depend upon them for appropriate wellness instruction and for appealing and persuasive wellness models. Wellness proper begins when self-determination begins.

These life-stage designations and descriptions are tentative, though the process they point to is real, chronological, and unavoidable for each individual. Each person goes through that process, though not necessarily at any set age. Each person is a separate and complicated individual who comes with his or her own history and has a very personal cycle of life to play out. Wellness can result when the individual does not just let life happen and submit to it but rather reaches out with determination and creatively seizes it.

The bulk of research on wellness and the life-stages is humanistic in nature. It is quite good and very thought-provoking. As is evident from this book, it has served as grist for my own reflections as I've attempted to integrate those insights with my understanding and experience of the Jewish and Christian religious traditions. There is much more to be said than I have managed to report in these few pages. Much yet remains to be done,[20] but for now at least a general outline has been drawn. Fill in the details as you tell your own story of wellness. Use the reflection questions to guide yourself.

NOTES

1. There are three essential articles: John G. Bruhn, Ph.D., F. David Cordova, Ed. D., James A. Williams, M.S.W., Raymond G. Fuentes, Jr., "The Wellness Process," *Journal of Community Health* 2 (#3, Spring 1977): 209-21: and John G. Bruhn, Ph. D., and F. David Cordova, Ed. D., "A Developmental Approach to Learning Wellness Behavior, Part I: Infancy to Early Adolescence," *Health Values* 1 (#6, Nov./Dec. 1977): 246-54; and "Part II: Adolescence to Maturity," *Health Values* 2 (#1, Jan./Feb. 1977): 16-21.

I differ from the position in these articles by making wellness distinct from physical health (visually, as a line parallel to the health/sickness continuum); Bruhn and his colleagues see health as the generic concept that includes everything on a spectrum from illness behavior to wellness behavior. One way to understand the difference is to realize that Bruhn has moved the discussion to the socio-cultural level of understanding, while I am attempting to integrate the socio-cultural dimension into the bio-medical dimension.

2. Annette Hollander, M.D., *How to Help Your Child Have a Spiritual Life: A Parent's Guide to Inner Development* (New York: A & W Publishers, 1980).

3. Catholic religious educators have often met parents who have abandoned the active practice of the Catholic faith but who insist on having their children receive the sacraments. These educators have felt genuine concern about the continuing instruction of these children and wondered whether these children would persevere in the active practice of the faith, since they had no impressive role-models in their daily lives. The revised rite for the baptism of children (1969) left an appropriate decision on this matter to individual conferences of bishops or individual bishops when the Sacred Congregation for Divine worship wrote: "In many countries parents are sometimes not ready for the celebration of baptism or they ask for their children to be baptized, although the latter will not afterwards receive a Christian education and will even lose the faith. Since it is not enough to instruct the parents and to inquire about their faith in the course of the rite itself, conferences of bishops may issue pastoral directives, for the guidance of parish priests, to determine a longer interval between birth and baptism"—n. 25, *Rite of Baptism for Children* (Washington, D.C.: United States Catholic Conference, 1969), p. 6.

4. Sharon Strassfeld and Michael Strassfeld, compilers and editors, *The Second Jewish Catalog* (Philadelphia: The Jewish Publication Society of America, 1976), p. 94.

5. See, for example, Philip S. Keane, *Sexual Morality: A Catholic Perspective* (New York: Paulist Press, 1977), for a scholarly presentation; or Nancy Hennesy Cooney with Anne Bingham, *Sex, Sexuality & You* (Dubuque, Ia.: William C. Brown, 1979), for material geared toward parents and teachers of the young.

6. In the Roman Catholic Archdiocese of Milwaukee, the archbishop has established the age of sixteen, or the junior/senior year of high-school education, as the normal time at which the sacrament of Confirmation may be received. He believes that it is at this age in a young person's life that the young person is capable of making a truly free choice. The archbishop's reasoning echoes the conclusions of the researchers in life-stages.

7. A more fully developed Christian wellness spirituality for the intermediate school age (nine to eleven years of age; grades four to six) is developed in the ten-episode audio-visual color filmstrip program *Growing in Wisdom, Maturity and Favor* (Milwaukee, Wis.: ROA Films, 1981). The Introductory Study Guide lists an extensive bibliography on wellness, spirituality, and the Christian Scriptures. A related audio-cassette program, *Stories from Luke to Grow By*, is available from NCR Cassettes, P. O. Box 281, Kansas City, MO 64141. That publisher also has a single cassette explaining the rationale for these last-mentioned approaches toward a wellness spirituality, *Children and Wellness*.

8. Daniel Levinson et al. *The Season of a Man's Life* (New York: Alfred A. Knopf, 1978).

9. Penelope Washbourn, *Becoming Woman* (New York: Harper & Row, 1977).

10. Gail Sheehy, *Passages* (New York: Bantam edition, 1977).

11. I have included a set of reflection questions keyed to presentations in a wellness retreat I regularly conduct that appears to be very popular among adults in all and varied stations of life. One specific retreat program is entitled "Francis of Assisi: Model of Lifelong Wellness." One doesn't have to be a Franciscan to like it.

The reflection questions are modeled after Levinson's and Washbourn's developments.

12. See Sheehy, *Passages*, pp. 295-96, and the entire chapter for details.

13. Washbourn, p. 46. The word *graceful* means "life-affirming, growth-promoting" in Washbourn's book. It is contrasted with *demonic*, which is life-denying, growth-defeating. The adjectives describe the two options open to women as they face the major decisions of life. They can make a demonic response (and choose death, stunted growth, etc.) or a graceful response (and choose life, enhanced growth—in my terms, wellness).

14. Levinson, *Seasons*, p. 30.

15. See p. 197, and then chapters 14 and 15, pages 209-54.

16. Washbourn, *Becoming Woman*, p. 134.

17. See p. 151.

18. Alfred McBride, "Adult Education: A Ministry to Life Cycles," *Religious Education* 72 (1977): 171-83. Both Levinson and McBride realize that Late (and Late-Late) Adulthood is still relatively uncharted. It is only in our lifetimes that life-expectancy has reached into the 70s and 80s. For this reason we need people of this age to tell us of their experiences, observations, and notions of the chief challenges of late and late-late adulthood. As a tentative description of the challenge of this stage of life, I have suggested "reconciliation leading to wisdom and holiness." The sketch in this chapter is developed in audio-visual format in "Aging," Episode Nine in *Christian Families* (Milwaukee, Wis.: ROA Filmstrips, 1980). Consult the Resource Guide for further references.

19. The School Sisters of Saint Francis, Office of Ministry, 1501 South Layton Boulevard, Milwaukee, WI 53215, have established a program for their retired Sisters: "Call of Retirement: Ministry of the Elders." The voluntary program has found a way to channel the energies of retired Sisters into a variety of "ministries." It is a model worthy of emulation.

20. Professor David O. Moberg of the Department of Sociology and Anthropology, Marquette University, has pursued research

along a related line, "spiritual well-being." One of his more recent publications has been with Patricia M. Brusek, "Spiritual Well-Being: A Neglected Subject in Quality of Life Research," *Social Indicators Research* 5 (1978): 303-23. See also David O. Moberg, ed., *Spiritual Well-Being: Sociological Perspectives* (Washington, D.C.: University Press of America, 1979).

REFLECTION GUIDE FOR CHAPTERS 1-4

There are five key elements by which to explore wellness, spiritual values, and religious beliefs:

1. knowing the meanings of life and having a purpose in life;
2. identifying life's authentic, satisfying, fulfilling, human joys and pleasures;
3. accepting responsibility for freedom of self-determination;
4. finding an effective, appropriate, and lasting source of motivation;
5. realizing the need for ongoing change in life, the need for occasional "conversion."

You can be terminally ill, mentally retarded, or permanently disabled and still have high-level wellness.

Or you can be perfectly healthy but have no purpose in living and therefore have no level of wellness.

Wellness is an ever-expanding experience of pleasurable and purposeful living which you and I, especially as motivated by spiritual values and religious beliefs, create and direct for ourselves in any way we choose. I use the following reflection questions during wellness retreats in which I allow participants an amount of time for personal, quiet reflection that is generally equal to the amount of time I devote to my four presentations: orientation to wellness (similar to the content of chapters 1 through 4); wellness in young adulthood, middle adulthood, and late adulthood (condensed in chapter 5). The reader is invited to use these reflection questions to develop an understanding of wellness, to identify the level of wellness possessed or desired, and to consider how to make wellness a lifelong pursuit.

PURPOSE IN LIFE

Wellness is directly related to your purpose in life. What is your goal, your whole reason for living? What do you want to do with your life?

What does *society* suggest as life's purpose: getting married? getting divorced? joining a convent? having a family? not having children? going to college? making a lot of money? other?

What does your *religion* suggest as life's purpose: saving your soul? avoiding sin? getting to heaven? making a lot of money? other?

What purpose does your *family* or *ethnic background* assign to life?

Who else has taught you about life's meaning, purpose, goal?

What have you decided for yourself on this topic?

PLEASURES, JOYS, SATISFACTION

Wellness depends upon your idea of life's authentically satisfying and fulfilling human pleasures. What is your "serum fun" level? Which of life's pleasures do you cherish: music? art? smoking? drinking? learning? reading? playing sports? work? sex? other?

Are these appropriate pleasures for human beings? Why? Which would you add (or subtract)?

Do you ever deny yourself or give up pleasures for any reason at any time? When? Why?

How much fun do you get out of life? What gives you greatest pleasure in living? the least?

How do you judge whether your happiness is truly satisfying and fulfilling in a human way?

FREEDOM, RESPONSIBILITY, DETERMINATION

Wellness hinges almost entirely on your freedom to determine the course of your life and to pursue that course. Only you can do wellness; no one can do it to or for you. You alone do wellness; but of course, you don't do it alone.

Who runs your life: God? parents? friends? your religion? the government? other? If combinations of these run your life, what is the combination?

Are you able to make a free decision? Who (or what) influences your decisions: advertising? an advisor? money? other?

Do you sometimes forego your own freedom out of respect for the freedom of another? E.g., can you give up smoking for a couple of hours to visit a non-smoking friend?

What "payoff" affects your decision-making: reward? promotion? publicity? tax incentive? a spiritual reward rather than a material one? other?

MOTIVATION

How did you get started in wellness? How do you keep it going? (This is motivation.)

Do you practice wellness because you *know* it is good for you? In other words, do you always behave according to what you know? Explain.

Do you practice wellness for an extrinsic reward—for example, reduced auto insurance for non-smokers?

How is your self-esteem? Do you have a high, or low, opinion of yourself?

Does your religion encourage you to practice wellness? E.g., what does your religion say about the body: good? bad? doesn't matter?

Do your religious (or secular) beliefs encourage fasting? What do you understand by fasting?

Do you take your religious beliefs seriously? all of them? How do you decide which beliefs to strengthen and which to cast aside? Are your beliefs related to wellness? From whom or what do you draw your beliefs?

CHANGE, CONVERSION

Are you comfortable with change in your personal life?
in society?

The Bureau of Labor says the average worker
changes jobs between seven and eleven times during the
working years of life. How many times have you
changed jobs? Why did you make the change?

The Hebrew word *shub* means redirection, or
getting one's head screwed on straight again, in the
modern vernacular. Has this ever happened to you? In
what circumstances?

The Greek work *metanoia* literally means "change of mind"; it also means "change of heart." Did you ever experience such a change? When? How?

The word *conversion* often carries negative overtones. It derives from the Latin version of the Hebrew and Greek words just mentioned. It means "broadening of horizons," "transformation of perspectives." A vernacular translation might be "wising up before it's too late." Is that experience familiar to you? Explain.

Draw yourself. Show how you look at your high levels of wellness; then contrast this picture with one of you at your lowest level of "worseness."

Where specifically did you locate your
wellness/"worseness" (e.g., feet, eyes, hair, mouth)? Does
this ever change? Could it? Under what conditions?

Do you have any idea of what threatens your
wellness? what lowers its level? Specify. What can you
do about that?

Write down some wellness teachings that you can
think of in your sacred literature: e.g., from Qoheleth,
or the Sayings of the Fathers, the Gospels, the Koran.

Are these teachings reflected in your day-to-day life-spaces (e.g., home, dorm, factory, office, hospital)? What changes would enhance the opportunity for daily wellness? Who can bring the change about?

Since you alone do wellness, but you don't do it alone, discuss some of these reflections with a significant other (e.g., brother, sister, spouse, friend).

REFLECTION GUIDE FOR CHAPTER 5

EARLY ADULTHOOD (18-40): FORMING AND LIVING OUT THE DREAM

Try to recall the earliest form of your dream(s) as described on page 116 of chapter 5. Jot it down here, briefly or in full. If it is applicable to you, also jot down the alterations to your dream, its evolution in this period if you prefer.

What was the source of your dream: vision, book, heroine/hero?

Did your dream have a supportive context: in family, in school, in church?

Were there obstacles or impediments to your dream (e.g., your marriage was arranged and predetermined; your choice of religious community was restricted)?

Did your dream become tyrannical? Was it inspirational?

Forming Mentor/Adviser Relationships
Who helped you form/live out your dream: man? woman? teacher? confessor? spiritual director? guidance counselor? relative? other?

How long did this relationship last? Continuously, or intermittently?

Was the mentor relationship warm and positive? or less than satisfying and negative?

Was there a "special man" or "special woman" in your life at this time (other than spouse or parent)? Was this person real, or fictional? living, or deceased? present and personally known, or distant and not personally known? What influences can you trace to this individual?

Forming an Occupation/Ministry
What did you want to do in life? Are you doing it now?
Were you able to do it then?

Did you have enough knowledge, judgment and
self-understanding to make a good choice of
occupation/ministry?

Was this a free choice? a "Hobson's choice"
(something "diplomatically" forced on a person)?

Was this occupation/ministry single and clearly
defined (e.g., business, teaching)? or was it hyphenated
(e.g., business in daytime to earn a living/teaching in
night hours for self-fulfillment)?

Forming a Vocation/State in Life
Was there ample opportunity to form adult peer
relationships with the opposite sex?

How did this choice relate to the choices of
occupation/ministry?

Summary:
What options for wellness do you have? What decisions
did you make? How did you live with the consequences
of your decision?

MIDDLE ADULTHOOD (40–60): INTEGRATING POLARITIES

This is a period for reappraising the past; modifying life-structures as necessary; and facing and integrating four basic polarities.

Integrating Young/Old (The Major Polarity)
How have you been "young" all your life: i.e., open to birth, growth, possibility, initiation, openness, energy, potential?

How have you yielded to being "old" in your life: i.e., yielded to termination, fruition, stability, structure, completion, death?

How have you re-balanced these polarities at this period of life? (Or how do you intend to re-balance them when you reach these ages?)

Integrating Destruction/Creation
How have you reworked painful feelings and experiences of daily living (in art? music? cooking? swimming?)?

Have you examined the tragic sense of life, the internal flaw (e.g., arrogance, pride, sense of omnipotence, stubbornness) that has laid you low in the past and can do it in the future?

Have you decided to cop out, or to seek a new balance of power and love?

What is your "soul-language?" How do you express your inner feelings, sentiments, experiences?

In sum, how have you re-balanced destructive and creative thrusts in your life at this age period? at various age periods?

Integrating Masculine/Feminine
Which are your masculine traits? How can you enhance them?

Which are your feminine traits? How can you enhance them?

Have you balanced the masculine/feminine polarity to your satisfaction?

Are you a creative person? Explore the areas of creativity in your life. Reflect upon how you promote and develop the creative talents in your life.

Integrating Attachment/Separateness
Much of life to this point is spent in "belonging" (e.g., family, community, clubs). Slowly now one begins to sense a need for separateness.

What is your "attachment index"—e.g., engaged, involved, seeking, plugged-in, rooted?

How do you construct and explore your imagined world?

What is your "separateness index"? I.e., do you have time and space for yourself? How active is your inner world: imagination, fantasy, play?

Meditation and reverie are healthy forms of extreme separateness. Do you indulge in them? How often? With what results?

Creativity works on the boundary of attachment and separateness. Are you satisfied with your level of creativity? Which area (e.g., attachment/separateness) might be able to improve your creativity?

How have you balanced your own needs with the needs of society (e.g. family/community/ministry)?

Summary:
These polarities exist during the entire life cycle. They can never be fully resolved or transcended. So long as life continues, no period marks the end of the opportunities and the burdens of further development.

LATE ADULTHOOD (60s AND ON): RECONCILIATION LEADING TO WISDOM AND HOLINESS

Since we are only now beginning to live into these ages, this segment of life remains as yet relatively uncharted. We must all explore the period: some by experience, others by anticipation.

Reconciliation
Just as Francis of Assisi at the end of his life came to terms with "Brother Ass" (as he called his body), so each of us needs to come to terms with various aspects of our life—the dream: fulfilled or still incomplete; the ministry, the vocation.

What was life all about till now?

Wisdom
How have I defined myself till now: by what I do? by
who I am? Does it make a difference?

How do I deal with society's emphasis on youth,
slimness, and other apparent slights toward aging?

Do I remember to substitute "head" for hands as
often as I can?

Have I arrived at some valuable insights that are
worth passing on to others?

Do I tell my story so the lives of others can be enriched?

Do I wear with pride the scars of risk and the stretch marks of revision?

Holiness
Now is the time to reap the fruits of separateness, to take the leisure to plumb the depths of the soul.
• What are the essential spiritual values you have identified in life?

- What form of prayer or meditation do you use in this stage of life? How does it relate to the forms you used earlier in life?

- What advice would you give a younger person that would help develop his or her spiritual life?

Now is the time to harvest the experiences that unfolded and continue to unfold in the dark nights of the soul.

- What can you share from your experiences of adversity? What lessons did you learn that would be worth passing on?

- How did you and do you overcome feelings of abandonment, loneliness, uselessness?

    Now is the time to bring to fruition the radical conversion begun in early adulthood. There are still choices to be made.
- Should one continue in familiar paths? or should one strike out on new adventures?

- Did you avoid or postpone change or conversion in early adulthood? middle adulthood? What difference does it make at this time of life?

And for those who reach late, late adulthood (80s and beyond) there are wellness challenges yet unheard of. Tell us your story, sing us your song, set our souls afire with desire for what is yet to come.

SELECT READINGS AND RESOURCES

Two very comprehensive reading lists on the subject of
   wellness are readily available in most bookstores:
   Popenoe, Cris. *Wellness: The YES! Bookshop Guide.*
   New York: Random House, 1977.
Ardell, Donald B. *High Level Wellness: An Alternative to
   Doctors, Drugs, and Disease.* Emmaus, Pa.: Rodale
   Press, 1977; New York: Bantam Books, 1979.
The select readings and resources list that follows
includes those books, articles, and resources especially
relevant to the wellness approach developed in this
book.

READINGS

Wellness
Bloomfield, Harold H., M.D., and Kory, Robert B.,
   M.S.W. *The Holistic Way to Health and Happiness: A
   New Approach to Complete Lifetime Wellness.* New
   York: Simon & Schuster, 1978. The authors devote
   about one-third of their book to discussing a
   humanistic understanding of the spiritual aspect of
   wellness.

Bruhn, John G., Ph. D.; Cordova, F. David, Ed. D.;
　Williams, James A., M.S.W., and Fuentes,
　Raymond G., Jr. "The Wellness Process," *Journal of
　Community Health* 2 (1977): 209-21. This and the
　following two articles describe the stages of lifelong
　wellness.
Bruhn, John G., Ph. D., and Cordova, F. David, Ed. D.
　"A Developmental Approach to Learning Wellness
　Behavior. Part I: Infancy to Early Adolescence,"
　Health Values 1 (1977): 246-54.
——————— . "Part II: Adolescence to Maturity,"
　Health Values 2 (1978): 16-21.
Bruhn, John G., and Wolf, Stewart. *The Roseto Story.*
　Norman: University of Oklahoma Press, 1979. Easy-
　reading report of a lengthy study on the Italian
　Community at Roseto, Pa., which demonstrated
　that stability and predictability of a community
　correlate better with low prevalence and incidence
　of coronary heart disease than the absence or low
　incidence of any of the conventionally accepted risk
　factors such as cholesterol.
Dunn, Halbert L., M.D. *High Level Wellness.* Arlington,
　Va.: Beatty, 1971. The "bible" of wellness, written
　by the movement's founding father. It is must
　reading for a proper understanding of the concept.
Travis, John W., M.D. *Wellness Workbook.* Wellness
　Resource Center, 42 Miller Avenue, Mill Valley,
　CA 94941; 1977. Travis combined insights from a
　variety of resources to compile this workbook.
　Since his understanding and practice continue to
　evolve, this workbook may simply represent his
　thinking in 1977, but it is very helpful to the
　beginner.

Spirituality
Caprio, Betsy. "Inner Passages," *St. Anthony Messenger*
　85 (February 1978), 13-18. Part of a projected book
　to be entitled *Maps of Growth*, this psychological

approach is rooted in Maslow from a Christian
spiritual perspective.
_____ . *Experiments in Growth*. Notre Dame:
Ave Maria Press, 1976. A "wellness workbook" by
another name.
The Jewish Encyclopedia and the *Encyclopedia Judaica*,
both generally available in the reference section of
libraries, are invaluable sources of information on
all aspects of Judaism.
Hollander, Annette, M.D. *How to Help Your Child Have
a Spiritual Life: A Parent's Guide to Inner
Development*. New York: A & W Publishers, 1980.
An excellent humanistic approach to the subject.
Le Déaut, Roger; Jaubert, Annie; and Hruby, Jurt. *The
Spirituality of Judaism*. Translated by Paul Barrett.
St. Meinrad, Ind.: Abbey Press, 1977. An
authoritative article excerpted and translated from
the famous *Dictionnaire de la Spiritualité* and
published in English as a booklet.
McBrien, Richard P. Chapter 28, "Christian
Spirituality," in *Catholicism*. Minneapolis: Winston
Press, 1980, pp. 1057-99. "Spirituality," says
McBrien on p. 1093, "has to do with one's style of
life, with one's way of experiencing God and of
shaping one's life on the basis of that experience."
By this definition, wellness can be a form of
spirituality. McBrien's overview of the history of
Christian spirituality and his review of
contemporary trends is excellent.
Meeks, Linda Bower. "The Role of Spiritual Health in
Achieving High Level Wellness," *Health Values* 1
(1977): 222-24. A rare article in a magazine that has
become increasingly oriented to the medical model
perspective on health and wellness.
Moberg, David O. "Social Indicators of Spiritual Well-
Being," in *Spiritual Well-Being for the Elderly*,

Thomas C. Cook, Jr., and James A. Thorson, eds.
Springfield, Ill.: Charles C. Thomas, 1979.
Moberg's quest is to analyze spiritual well-being
quantitatively.
Popenoe, Cris. *Inner Development.* Published by Yes!
Inc., 1035 31st Street, N.W., Washington, D.C.
20007; 1979. Distributed by Random House. An
excellent annotated bibliography on various
approaches to spirituality.

RESOURCES

Body & Soul (Alchemy Communications, P.O. Box 257,
Oregon, IL 61061). A monthly newsletter exploring
the tensions between the sacred and the secular,
between sensuality and spirituality, between body
and soul. Sample copy on request.
Greater Milwaukee Conference on Religion and Urban
Affairs, 1442 North Farwell Avenue, Suite 208,
Milwaukee, WI 53202. Since 1977, the GMCRUA
has supported a Wholistic Health Care Task Force
to assist believers in the Milwaukee area in their
pursuit of wellness. It has met with modest but
measurable success. Send for information about
available bibliographies and other materials.
Shantivanam—House of Prayer, Route 1, Easton, KS
66020. Father Ed Hays, priest-hermit of the Kansas
City, Kansas, diocese, publishes a monthly
newsletter called "The Forest Letter" (*Shantivanam*
in Sanskrit means "forest of peace") and has issued
two books: *Prayers for the Domestic Church* and
Prayers for the Servants of God. Write for free
information about these materials and about visits
to the farm for prayer and retreat.
The Wellness Kit, containing a Personal Wellness Profile
and Family Wellness Profile, is available for the
asking from Aid Association for Lutherans,
Appleton, WI 54919.

Additional materials on wellness and spirituality by the author of this book:

Audio-cassettes from NCR Cassettes, P. O. Box 281, Kansas City, MO 64141:
Spirituality and High Level Wellness
Wellness in Families
The Energized Family
Children and Wellness
Francis: Model of Lifelong Wellness
Ministry and Wellness, which includes: "A Framework for Understanding," "Holistic Health Care and Preventive Medicine," "Wellness: Caring for our Human Spirit," "Making Life and Work One," or "Wellness in the Workplace," "Developing a Psychology of Self." An accompanying printed folder contains bibliography and charts.
Reading the New Testament Healing Texts, which includes: "Contemporary Healing: A Framework for Understanding," "The Uniqueness of Jesus the Healer," "Reading the Healing Stories Part I and Part II."
Parish Wellness, which includes: "What is Wellness?", "The Meaning of Life," "The Joys of Life," "Freedom of Self-determination," "The Community and Wellness," "Wellness in Parish Renewal," "Wellness: A Biblical Spirituality."

Correspondence-course program with exercises:
Developing an Holistic Spirituality, University of the South, Sewanee, TN 37375.

Filmstrips from ROA Films, 1696 N. Astor Street, Milwaukee, WI 53202:
Christian Families, a set of ten audio-visual, color/sound filmstrips featuring actual case-studies of real families and their real concerns. Topics: "Getting

Married," "Starting a Family," "Parenting," "A
Single Parent Family," "Being Single," "Childless
Marriage," "Two Families as One," "Serious
Injury," "Aging," "Death and Dying." A program
to enrich family wellness.

Growing in Wisdom, Maturity, and Favor, a set of ten
audio-visual, color/sound filmstrips for the nine- to
eleven-year-old (grades four to six), illustrating the
key elements of a wellness spirituality based on
Luke's gospel. To be released in 1981.

DATE DUE

MAR 8 '94			